PROPHETIC OPERATIONS

Journey Into The World Of The Prophets

by

JONAS CLARK

A SPIRIT OF LIFE CLASSIC

PROPHETIC OPERATIONS
Journey Into The World Of The Prophets
ISBN 1-886885-11-7

Copyright © 2001 by Jonas Clark

Published by Spirit of Life Publishing
27 West Hallandale Beach Blvd.
Hallandale, Florida
33009-5437, U.S.A.
(954) 456-4420

02 03 04 05 06 07 ♦ 07 06 05 04 03 02

ABOUT
THE AUTHOR

The anointing on his life is both bold and strong. Jonas' great passion is to take this gospel of the kingdom into all the world. Fortitude and God's grace have taken the ministry international, carrying a message of divine impact and reform for this generation into over twenty-three nations. Jonas is...

pioneer of the Global Cause Network (GNC), a fellowship of over 58 churches around the world of like precious faith.

senior editor of The Ambassador Journal (www.catchlife.org), the New Apostolic Voice for the 21st Century. An internet magazine and prophetic journal sent to thousands of leaders in more than 62 countries.

a prolific writer who has authored many books with an apostolic and prophetic voice that are catching the attention of the church.

founder of Spirit of Life Publishing which provides critical learning resources, educational and informational materials throughout the nations.

pioneer of The Harvest Strategy, a reforming ministry structure for city-wide evangelism.

founder of Spirit of Life Ministries in Hallandale Beach, Florida an apostolic training center.

As a reformer, his desire is to see the nations of the world impacted and changed by the power of God. Jonas has been in the ministry for seventeen years. He is blessed with his beautiful wife Rhonda and three daughters Natasha, Nichole and Natalie.

THIS BOOK
IS DEDICATED TO

All the ministry gifts around the world that hunger and thirst for prophetic accuracy and holiness.

Keep on praying,

and

To you, the prophetic church!

"And he gave some, apostles; and some, prophets; and some, evangelists; and some, pastors and teachers; {12} For the perfecting of the saints, for the work of the ministry, for the edifying of the body of Christ" (Ephesians 4:11-12 KJV).

CONTENTS

Prophets will not tolerate church games and they detest religious politics. The prophet may give personal prophecies, but his revelation gifting goes way beyond personal prophecy. God is raising up a prophetic people who have been delivered from the "fear of men" and who are not "men pleasers."

There has been a restoration of the prophets and a prophetic release in the earth. God is calling, training, activating, and releasing the prophets with a great work in this hour. With this restoration comes a great assignment designed to discredit the true prophetic gift.

A presumptuous prophet is one who thinks that God wants to speak all the time to people according to his faith only and not according to the will of the Lord. If you prophesy by faith alone, then you are in danger of tapping into a spirit of divination. The prophet, who has not been granted permission to prophesy and yet does, is guilty of sin.

Power, money, prestige, honor, promotion, and enticements with flattering smooth sayings are all demonic assignments designed to pull on any common ground that might be in the heart of God's prophetic ministers.

The prophetic ministry is not always liked or received. Oftentimes it even violates public opinion. Micaiah is a great example of God preparing a prophet to speak to a coveting King.

The prophetic tongue that is not flowing through an accurate prophetic operation can release iniquity, lawlessness, and prophetic defilement. However, prophets who are flowing accurately can bring great blessing to the body of Christ. God uses prophets to announce, activate, impart, confirm, and unlock times and seasons.

Our society is filled with those that come into our churches who have formerly opened themselves up to New Age Mysticism, witchcraft, the occult, and spiritualism. To protect the flock from false anointings and familiar spirits, there is a proper order in which the Holy Spirit likes to flow.

INTRODUCTION

Prophetic Operations is a journey into the prophetic ministry. We will at tempt to clear up some confusion between true prophet or false prophet by taking a look at true prophetic gifts with potentially false prophetic operations.

This book addresses some of the puzzling questions that pastors have asked me concerning prophetic ministry, including it's pitfalls. I am certainly not an expert in prophetic ministry, yet I believe strongly that God has a prophetic flow. My intentions in writing this book are not to stir controversy; we only "know in part and prophesy in part." In this work we submit just one part for your examination and judgment.

We will explore the differences between prophecy by faith and prophecy by unction while reviewing the results of each. We will look at prophesying by the Holy Spirit, prophesying by a spirit of divination, and prophetic defilement by smooth sayings. In addition, we will ask the question, "Why does it seem that God changes His mind in personal prophetic ministry?"

In the final chapter we will review some earmarks of a spiritist. I pray that this book ministers to you.

From South Florida,

Jonas Clark

CHAPTER 1

THE PROPHET'S MINISTRY

Prophets will not tolerate church games and they detest religious politics. The prophet may give personal prophecies, but his revelation gifting goes way beyond personal prophecy. God is raising up a prophetic people who have been delivered from the "fear of men" and who are not "men pleasers."

The prophet's ministry is different than the pastoral ministry. The pastor has great compassion for the sheep, but the prophet is gifted in a much different way. We need all the five-fold ministry gifts functioning in the church.

> "And he gave some, apostles; and some, prophets; and some, evangelists; and some, pastors and teachers." (Ephesians 4:11 KJV)

They are all very important. We need the apostle; he is an establisher and a builder. We need the prophet; he is a mouthpiece of God. We need the evangelist; we need to focus on reaching the lost.

If you spend time with an evangelist, you will see signs, wonders and miracles, but the job of an evangelist is not to disciple you. You need a pastor and a teacher for that.

CHOSEN INSTRUMENTS

"Before I formed thee in the belly I knew thee; and before thou camest forth out of the womb I sanctified thee, and I ordained thee a prophet unto the nations." (Jeremiah 1:5 KJV)

Prophets are chosen instruments of God that are set apart to speak. Their ministries are different and distinct. Prophets are not always waiting to be led; they know by the Spirit where they are going and exactly what they are called to do and to say. They are sent to speak.

Prophets are sent by God with the Word. They will not tolerate church games, and they detest religious politics. Unfortunately they're not always very good statesmen. They walk into the room and want to speak the Word of God, even if it is not popular or religiously correct. Prophets don't care much about public opinion. They are more concerned with 'what saith the Spirit of God.' They sometimes seem to be driven by the Holy Spirit with an incredible sense of urgency.

> PROPHETS ARE THE MOST
> SPIRITUALLY SENSITIVE OF ALL THE
> FIVE-FOLD MINISTRY GIFTS

When you walk too close to a prophet, there could be things about him that may make you feel uncomfortable, yet there are some things about his ministry gift that he cannot avoid. Just the very nature of the prophet's gift can be confrontational and very bold at times. It's not that a prophet is intentionally confrontational; it's because of the spiritual realm they operate in. Understand the prophet's ministry gift, function, equipment and operation. When you value it you can benefit from it.

In contrast, the pastor seems easier to love. Everyone loves him, and he loves the sheep. A pastor's calling is to nurture, console and protect. You can bite him and he will take it. But if you bite the prophet, watch-out, he might just bite you back.

UNDERSTANDING ORDER

The prophet's gift really comes alive during times of spiritual war and when things are out of order. His entire focus is to hear from God and speak into the situation. Because prophets are stewards of the mysteries of God (Ephesians 3:4-5) they will get before the altar of God in prayer and cry out to God for revelation. *Whereas a pastor may take the needs of the people to God in prayer, the prophet will take the word of the Lord to the people.*

Often the young prophet does not make a very good pastor. Why? Because of the difference in gift functions. Prophets must work toward mercy and compassion where a pastor is already gifted with those qualities. This is not to say that prophets cannot pastor, they can.

Historically, prophets have been traveling ministries because the church did not know how to relate to the operation of their gift. Today prophets are not called by God to be outside the local church, but have been given as a foundation gift to the church (Ephesians 2:20). Because many churches closed the doors to the prophet, God...

♦ gathered them together in prophetic companies where they were accepted

♦ sent them to pioneer and start new churches until the body of Christ was ready to receive their gift

♦ used them to start prophetic schools where emerging prophets were trained, confirmed, activated and released.

ORDER GIFTS

Prophets, similar to apostles, are order gifts. They are foundational and deal with belief systems (Ephesians 2:20). When a prophet enters a room or when someone stands in front of him, he immediately knows if anything is out of order. That's the revelation gifting going off inside of him. *Prophets are the most spiritually sensitive of all the five-fold ministry gifts.* So if there is anything out of order in the church or out of order in your life, he will pick it up in the Spirit. It's not suspicion. Suspicion comes out of the soul through carnal reasoning.

Suspicion is suspecting guilt, wrongs or harms with little or no supporting evidence.

7

The prophetic gift has nothing to do with suspicion or soulish workings but operates out of a knowing by the Holy Spirit.

THE SEER

In the Old Testament, the prophet was referred to as a seer. This seeing ability is like drawing back a curtain and being enabled to see what is hidden behind it. One prophet said that being able to see prophetically was like pulling himself up on top of a wall and then looking on the other side.

> "See, I have this day set thee over the nations and over the kingdoms, to root out, and to pull down, and to destroy, and to throw down, to build, and to plant." (Jeremiah 1:10 KJV)

One cannot root out, pull down, and destroy what cannot be seen. The word seer (*ra'ah*) means a beholder of visions. In Israel the term seer was the title given a prophet (1 Samuel 9:9).

DIVINE GUIDANCE

Appointed as overseers of nations, prophets receive divine guidance. Divine guidance for the nations is a high level operation of the prophetic gift. The pastor seldom receives that function because he doesn't need it, but a prophet surely does. It's a wonderful operation because it declares God's will for the nations. The prophet speaks what the Spirit has to say to the churches *and* the nations. Prophetic operations release...

hope

purpose

life

warnings

guidance.

Prophetic guidance means...

the pointing of the way

to direct on course

to give instruction

to provide insight.

A LIVING WORD

Prophets are gifted to bring forth a living (rhema) word to the church.

"He that hath an ear, let him
hear what the Spirit saith unto
the churches." (Revelation 2:29
KJV)

We need to listen to what the Spirit is
saying to the church, not just what the
Spirit has said. We need the freshness of
the revelation that comes through the
prophet's gift. Without that freshness we die
a religious boring death and are not spiritually relatable to our generation. So we need
the prophetic voice to come into the earth
that we might have a *"living word"* imparted
into our lives. Without the life provided by
the prophetic voice the church would be like
the dry bones in Ezekiel's vision.

God desires to raise up a prophetic
church. Not just a single lone prophet, but
a prophetic people. It is important that the
world hears the Word of the Lord. But they
have to hear it with power and with a re-
freshing that comes from a prophetic anointing. We need a prophetic people who have
been delivered from the "fear of men" and
who are not "men pleasers."

A ROTOR ROOTER MINISTRY

"See, I have this day set thee
over the nations and over the
kingdoms, to root out, and to

pull down, and to destroy, and
to throw down, to build, and to
plant." (Jeremiah 1:10 KJV)

In this verse, nations are symbolic of the
natural realm, and kingdoms are symbolic
of the spiritual realm. Prophets are also
called to root out. This is a reason why the
prophetic operation is sometimes not well
liked. To root out means to lay hold of the
root of a thing and pull. The prophet is
called to root out. He is called to pull down.
He is called to destroy. He is called to over-
throw. *Prophets are God's spiritual reformers.* To reform means to bring about change.
Many try to get rid of the prophet or close
his mouth before he gets to do what he really likes to do best. He is called to build
and plant. However there are many spiritual obstacles that must be dealt with first.
The prophet is gifted to prepare the way
through his rotor rooter challenge of spiritual opposition. One reason some feel uncomfortable with prophetic operations is
because of the results of his prayers. What
the prophet attacks through intercession in
the Spirit will always manifest in the natural. If he attacks rebellion then any common ground of rebellion will manifest in the
people. But rather than stop his rooting out
intercession, we should continue to press

in and let him finish his work. Once he is finished his gift will help opens the heavens to us.

PROPHETIC PROGRESSION

Sometimes when the prophet speaks, people will get stirred and offended. Offenses are the bait of Satan used to unplug you from relationships. If you are being challenged, perhaps the Holy Spirit is trying to prepare you for your future. We are in a time where the church is being prophetically challenged. Roots of binding religious tradition are being pulled out.

We have been sitting in our comfort zones for so long that when the prophetic anointing operates it stirs us and makes us very uncomfortable. God is bringing His prophets forth again. The church has prophetically progressed from...

be healed, to be taught

from be blessed, to be changed.

Everybody likes to be healed, taught, and blessed because it requires little on the part of the hearer. But the restoration of the prophetic to the church will move us into a governmental authority that will require more of us.

PERSONAL PROPHECY

Some people think that a prophet must give personal prophecies to qualify to walk in the office of a prophet. That's partially true. He will give personal prophecies, but his revelation gifting goes far beyond personal prophecy only. *Personal prophecy is the lowest prophetic operation of the true prophet.* Prophets also...

♦ are forerunners who make a way for greater things to come (Matthew 3:3)

♦ deal with spiritual climates (Jeremiah 1:10)

♦ turn people from sin to holiness (Jeremiah 23:21-22)

♦ are intercessory (Jeremiah 27:18)

♦ turn the hearts of fathers and sons (Malachi 4:5-6)

♦ challenge traditions of men and religion (Matthew 3:9-10)

♦ are stewards of the mysteries of God (Ephesians 3:5)

♦ carry lamentations, mourning and woe (intercession burdens) (Ezekiel 2:10)

♦ are foretellers of things to come (Amos 3:7)

♦ contend with false prophets (1 Kings 18:19)

♦ challenge demonic territorial guards (Acts 13:7)

♦ speak to the nations (Jeremiah 1:5)

SUMMARY

☐ Prophets are the most spiritually sensitive of all the fivefold ministry gifts.

☐ Divine guidance for the nations is a high level operation of the prophetic gift.

☐ Prophets are God's spiritual reformers.

☐Prophets, similar to apostles, are order gifts. They are foundational and deal with belief systems (Ephesians 2:20).

☐Suspicion is suspecting guilt, wrongs or harms with little or no supporting evidence.

DIVINE GUIDANCE FOR THE NATIONS IS A HIGH LEVEL OPERATION OF THE PROPHETIC GIFT

In the next chapter we will explore the risk of a prophetic defilement that will deter true prophetic operations.

CHAPTER 2

PROPHETIC RELEASE

There has been a restoration of the prophets and a prophetic release in the earth. God is calling, training, activating, and releasing the prophets with a great work in this hour. With this restoration comes a great assignment designed to discredit the true prophetic gift.

Have you noticed how many in the body of Christ are sick? Have you also noticed the lack of true spiritual discernment and prophetic life?
With the restoration of prophetic operations is the potential of a prophetic defilement. The definition of defilement means...

to make unholy

to blend an unholy mixture

to render profane

to make unclean.

Could defilement be keeping us from coming into the unity of the faith? Could defilement be caused by not properly discerning the Lord's ministry gifts? Could the prophets themselves be part of the problem?

Once I was with several people praying when I began to hear some of them prophesy. I was uneasy in my spirit because there was something that wasn't quite right. I just couldn't put my finger on it. The Spirit of God began to talk to me saying, "There are things in their lives that they are doing that are defiling them. There is no longer a desire for holiness; they have a blend, an unholy mixture." That unholy mixture is called defilement. It can be likened to the strange fire that the sons of Aaron brought into the temple that brought God's judgment (Leviticus 10:1).

Throughout this book I will be weaving in the thought of an unholy mixture as *the* demonic assignment sent to pollute the body of Christ and discredit the prophetic gift.

A true prophetic anointing will release a conviction of sin and a hunger for holiness. When the prophetic anointing came on the prophet Isaiah he recognized his need for holiness when he said, "Woe is me! for I am undone; because I am a man of unclean lips, and I dwell in the midst of a people of unclean lips: for mine eyes have seen the King, the LORD of hosts" (Isaiah 6:5 KJV).

A PROPHETIC RESTORATION

There has been a restoration of the prophets and a prophetic release in the earth. God is calling, training, activating, and releasing the prophets with a great work in this hour. He is also restoring the apostles who the prophets must identify and work together with.

There was a time, not too long ago, when we thought that all we had in the church were pastors who were also the teachers. We didn't recognize that there was a separate teaching gift. Yes, we believed there were evangelists, but there certainly were not any prophets and there absolutely were not any apostles.

The word teaches us that God has a five-fold group of ministry gifts given to the church of apostles, prophets, evangelists, pastors and teachers (Ephesians 4:11). With the restoration of all five gifts working together, we can expect to see at least five things happen.

> 1.) There will be a release of true prophets, speaking with true prophetic utterances throughout the church.

2.) The devil will counteract the prophetic restoration with a release of false prophets speaking with false prophetic utterances.

3.) There will be a danger of true prophets speaking with false prophetic utterances. These false prophetic utterances will release defilement and discredit the true prophetic gift.

4.) There will be a strong prophetic release that will make a way for the restoration of God's apostolic spiritual government in the local church.

5.) There will be a separation of true prophets and false prophets into different companies leading to a prophetic confrontation.

PROPHETIC CONFRONTATION

We can see a pattern for this prophetic confrontation between the true and the false by looking at Jeremiah's ministry. The prophets in the city failed to...

address sin

pursued idols

concentrated on accumulating
wealth

pursued power

did nothing to turn the people
from sin toward God.

Because of neglect and self-centered idolatry, God anointed Jeremiah to confront
them. Let's take a look.

> "Mine heart within me is bro-
> ken because of the prophets; all
> my bones shake; I am like a
> drunken man, and like a man
> whom wine hath overcome, be-
> cause of the LORD, and because
> of the words of his holiness."
> (Jeremiah 23:9 KJV)

Jeremiah speaking by the Spirit of God
says, "My heart is broken because of the
prophets." Notice he didn't say false prophets. The word prophet means a prophetic
voice. In other words, Jeremiah's heart was
broken because of the false prophetic words
that the prophets were speaking.

Jeremiah declares that all his bones shook and he was like a drunken man. Bones refer to structure. The shaking of the bones refers to the arranging or realigning of the structure of the church. There is an anointing on this prophet. He has heard the Word of the Lord and he is about to enter into a spiritual war. The anointing of the Spirit is on him and he began to shake. He looked like a drunken man. He had the Word of the Lord in his mouth and was ready to address the other prophets in the land.

CHARISMATIC ZEAL

When you read the book of Judges, you find that there are seven great apostasies that were present in the land. In response God raised up seven judges or great deliverers including Samson to deal with the people. The church is a lot like Samson with a lot of Charismatic zeal, little power and limited character.

One day three thousand of the tribe of Judah came to help the Philistines bind Samson. The religious spirits are full of the law and always want to bind up the church. Because of Samson's sin of laying his head in the lap of Delilah (representative of the world), Samson was blinded and lost his sight and had no more revelation from God. His hair was cut, symbolic of his strength and he was bound. A little lad led the great Samson into a temple where they made sport of him.

PERSONAL PROPHECY IS THE LOWEST PROPHETIC OPERATION OF THE TRUE PROPHET

A great era manifested itself after Samson's death. God raised up Samuel and began to restore the prophetic voice. It was also Samuel, God's prophet, who anointed David as king.

We will see this prophetic rise again. This is why the prophetic church is coming alive. Samson (worldliness) has been reigning in the church. Now God is releasing the prophetic church because we are the generation that will see the coming of the Lord. Because of this prophetic restoration, the enemy is countering by releasing defilement into the land. He is attacking us with confusion while attempting to abort the prophetic purposes of God.

SPIRITUAL ADULTERY

"For the land is full of adulterers; for because of swearing the

land mourneth; the pleasant
places of the wilderness are
dried up, and their course is
evil, and their force is not
right." (Jeremiah 23:10 KJV)

The Spirit of God is saying that because
of the pollution of the prophetic ministry
the "land was full of adulterers." Serving God
in spirit and truth means to serve him out
of a pure heart. Spiritual fornication and
idolatry separates you from God. One be-
comes a spiritual adulterer when he puts
something between himself and God. *Forsaking God for something or someone else
is spiritual adultery.* Because of yoking with
idols and idolatry, there are shakings and
rumblings coming forth into many lives.

So the land became full of adulterers,
mourned and lacked fresh revelation. What
brought about this curse? It was the forsaking of God because of a resistance to commitment, self-centeredness, unholy living,
idolatry, and seeking for entertainment and
blessing only.

HARD HEAVENS

"And thy heaven that is over thy
head shall be brass..."
(Deuteronomy 28:23 KJV)

Most of us are familiar with the list of blessings in the book of Deuteronomy. Let's take a look at one of the curses.

Why was the land cursed? Because the people had forsaken God. As a result of forsaking God, the heavens that were over their heads were as brass.

Those who have done any ministering at all find that as they go from one church to the next there is such a difference in the spiritual climates. Some churches or even cities are wonderful to preach in, while others are hard as rocks with brass heavens. A brazen heaven is a spiritual climate that must be plowed through strong intercession and militant preaching. Hard heavens are the result of...

sin

rebellion

demonic influence

strong territorial spirits

principalities

a turning toward idolatry

forsaking God.

Hard heavens have little revelation. When you pray it feels like your prayers hit the ceiling and fall back into your lap. You prophesy and the words come out of your mouth and seem to fall to the ground.

> "... the earth under you shall be
> as iron" (Deuteronomy 28:23).

When the earth is like iron nothing will grow. It's because of the curse that the land was spiritually defiled. Where there is no growth there is no spiritual maturity.

America is beginning to see the results of these curses caused by rebellion. As soon as we took prayer out of our schools, we replaced it with lawlessness. Whenever we reject that which comes from God, we have to settle with the opposite. If we don't want the Prince of Peace, we get the prince of calamity.

FROM HOLINESS
TO DEFILEMENT

> "For both prophet and priest
> are *profane*; yea, in my house
> have I found their wickedness,
> saith the LORD." (Jeremiah
> 23:11 KJV Italics added)

26

The word profane means "threshold." A threshold is the divider between two rooms. When you walk through a doorway there is a metal or wooden threshold on the floor that separates one side of the room from the other. There is a spiritual threshold that is a separation between the Holy and the unholy. So when one profanes they step across the threshold from holiness into defilement.

This scripture teaches us that the prophets had forsaken their holy operations and crossed the threshold from holy living into a prophetic defilement. Both prophet and priest were living in sin. Their defilement hindered God's plan for their lives, the church and released judgment on the land.

From studying this scripture we discover two different prophetic operations. First, we see that Jeremiah was so different from the other prophets in the land. Jeremiah managed to live a holy life whereas the others fell into sin and idolatry. Secondly, we discover that there were true prophetic operations in the land and false prophetic operations in the land. The true was releasing blessing and the false was causing a defilement.

"Wherefore their way shall be unto them as slippery ways in the darkness: they shall be driven on, and fall therein: for I

will bring evil upon them, even
the year of their visitation, saith
the LORD." (Jeremiah 23:12
KJV)

God pronounced that these prophets
would have slippery ways and a lack of true
spiritual discernment because of their life-
styles. They had no discernment because
they were walking in darkness having defiled themselves.

"And I have seen folly in the
prophets of Samaria" (Jeremiah
23:13 KJV).

Folly refers to...

foolishness

foolish actions

foolish beliefs

one void of spiritual discernment.

These prophets sounded good, looked
good, yet were void of spiritual stability. They
were doing foolish things and there was no

balance in their lives. Their idolatry produced a spiritual defilement which caused them to lose true spiritual discernment.

> "they prophesy by Baal and caused my people to go astray" (Jeremiah 23:13 KJV).

Can you imagine Jeremiah telling the prophets that they were prophesying by Baal? Baal is the spirit of divination. A true prophet of God will not allow the people to go astray. Even if their heart is not open to him, he will speak to them without compromise. *Prophetic defilement is the assignment used to take out the prophet.*

SUMMARY

☐A true prophetic gift will release a conviction of sin and a hunger for holiness.

☐Forsaking God for something or someone else is idolatry.

☐Prophetic defilement is the assignment used to take out the prophet.

☐Defilement means to make un-

holy, to blend an unholy mixture, to render profane, or to
make unclean.

☐God has a five-fold group of
ministry gifts given to the
church of apostles, prophets,
evangelists, pastors and teachers (Ephesians 4:11).

In the next chapter we are going to discuss the importance of waiting for the unction of the Holy Spirit. The prophet, who
has not been granted permission to prophesy and yet does, is guilty of sin.

CHAPTER 3

PROPHETIC UNCTIONS

A presumptuous prophet is one who thinks that God wants to speak all the time to people according to his faith only and not according to the will of the Lord. If you prophesy by faith alone, then you are in danger of tapping into a spirit of divination. The prophet, who has not been granted permission to prophesy and yet does, is guilty of sin.

When you prophesy make sure that you get an unction from the Holy Ghost — *first*. This is how we keep defilement out of our ministries and out of the land.

"Knowing this first, that no prophecy of the scripture is of any private interpretation. {21} For the prophecy came not in old time by the will of man: but

31

holy men of God spake as they
were moved by the Holy Ghost."
(2 Peter 1:20-21 KJV)

I had a man tell me once that he had
received a revelation from God. I asked him
to share it with me and he said, "It is too
deep. No church is ready for it." I said,
"Brother, you need to be very careful with
that. If you have a revelation from God, you
need to let us hear it and let the prophets
judge it. Don't come across with this stuff
saying that the church isn't ready for it. If
God has revealed something, then He wants
it to enter the earth. Let's hear it, examine
it, and let the prophets judge it."

All prophecies need to be judged, exam-
ined, and weighed against the scriptures (1
John 4:1).

Prophets and prophecies are fallible.
Scripture says that we see through a glass
darkly (1 Corinthians 13:12). If prophets
and prophecies were accurate all the time,
then the people would be following prophets instead of Jesus.

PROPHECY
BY THE WILL OF MAN

Prophecy of God was never spoken by
the will of man, that is to say by man's will.
If one prophesies by faith only, without an

unction, then they are prophesying according to their own wills and not God's will. Prophesying is not something that you do first by faith. It is not by your will alone. Your faith is not making it happen. Faith is involved, yes, but you are not making the prophetic utterance come by your faith alone. Understand this and protect yourself from defilement. Nor is this about emotion, it's about unction. Let's look at the pattern. Men spoke as they were...

moved

propelled

compelled

prompted by the Holy Spirit.

Prophetic utterances are always accompanied with an unction. If there is no unction, then you are prophesying by your faith alone. If you prophesy by faith alone, then you are in danger of tapping into a spirit of divination.

Divination is trying to foretell the future by occult means.

It is very important to know that prophecy should come after you receive the unction to speak.

> Unction is the permission of the
> Holy Spirit to prophesy.

After you receive the "unction," *then* let your faith kick in and let the prophecies come forth. The five-step process for prophetic release is...

1. God desires to speak

2. Holy Spirit gives an unction

3. Prophet's faith lays hold of the unction

4. Prophet speaks

5. Utterance (prophecy) is judged.

A PROPHETIC MANTEL

I noticed some people who were praying together recently. As I was listening, it appeared that many in the group were prophesying. What was so striking to me was that I had never heard these people prophesy before. So what was it that was different in this particular group? There was a man with a prophetic mantel in their midst. The reason they were able to prophesy to that degree was because they had picked up on his prophetic gift. This is what happened to King Saul when he came into the presence of the prophets (1 Samuel 19:24). Let's look at Ezekiel's release to prophesy to understand this more fully.

> "So I prophesied as I was commanded" (Ezekiel 37:7 KJV).

In this verse Ezekiel, a mature prophet of God, understands that he is not to prophesy until the Lord releases him to do so. We too can learn from this.

It is all right to sense the prophetic anointing and to hear, but don't speak "Thus saith the Lord" unless God tells you to through an unction or prompting by the Holy Spirit. If we begin to prophesy by faith without an unction, (outside of God's permission) we are in danger of tapping into a spirit of divination. This is a hard truth! If we tap into a spirit of divination, we release witchcraft over the people and ourselves. I spend a lot of time discussing the works of witchcraft in my book *Exposing Spiritual Witchcraft*.1

DEALING WITH EVILDOERS

Let's continue to review Jeremiah's prophetic operations as he deals with the false prophets in his territory.

> "I have seen also in the prophets of Jerusalem an horrible thing: they commit adultery, and walk in lies: they strengthen also the hands of evildoers, that none doth return from his wickedness: they are all of them unto me as Sodom, and the inhabitants thereof as Gomorrah." (Jeremiah 23:14 KJV)

This verse describes the pitiful condition of God's prophets who were...

committing adultery

lying

strengthening the hands of evil doers.

How do prophets strengthen the hands of evildoers? By prophesying that all is well to a person who is living in sin. God describes this same strengthening of evildoers when he declares, "they have seduced my people, saying, Peace; and there was no peace; and one built up a wall, and, lo, others daubed it with untempered mortar" (Ezekiel 13:10 KJV).

PROPHETIC PULL

Once during a powerfully anointed service I asked God if he wanted me to prophesy to the people. I could tell that the people were pulling on me for a word. The Spirit of God said, "No." Now could I have prophesied anyway? The answer is yes. But I would have been in rebellion. If you prophesy without God's permission you can tap into a familiar spirit.

Much of what we watch on Christian television is nice, looks, and sounds good, but not everything said is necessarily from God. Therefore God has put the responsibility into our lap to judge what is accurate and what is not.

> "Therefore thus saith the LORD of hosts concerning the prophets; Behold, I will feed them with wormwood, and make them drink the water of gall: for from the prophets of Jerusalem is profaneness (defilement) gone forth into all the land." (Jeremiah 23:15 KJV)

Because these prophets refused to repent, God allowed them to drink the water of their own rebellion. But notice what God tells us, "from the prophets is profaneness gone into all the land." It is this profaneness that all prophets must guard themselves from.

God is raising up prophets and a prophetic people. We need to be careful and wise. We need to understand the ways of the Spirit and the Word of God. We need to recognize the difference between...

the Holy from the profane

the true from the false

the clean from the unclean.

We need to leave the realm of low level prophetic utterance and enter a high level of spiritual capacity. *When prophets violate holy living they open themselves up to idolatry.*

A HYPOCRITICAL INQUIRER

What happens if the person who approaches a prophet for a prophetic word has idolatry in his heart? Does this effect the prophet's operations? Let's look to Ezekiel's ministry for some insight to this question.

38

"And the word of the LORD came unto me, saying, Son of man, these men have set up their idols in their heart, and put the stumblingblock of their iniquity before their face: should I be inquired of at all by them?" (Ezekiel 14:2-3 KJV)

The word of the Lord had come to Ezekiel. There were men standing in front of him. They may have been elders in the church. They may have been around for awhile but God says that they had idols in their heart. Ezekiel may not have known of their idolatry but God revealed that something in their hearts was not right.

As they approached Ezekiel for a prophetic word God's question was, "Should I answer them?" Good question. Let's look into this. If someone comes up to the prophet with iniquity in their heart, and are inquiring of the Lord for a prophetic word, God is asking the question, "Should I answer them?" Let's see what God says to Ezekiel to find the answer to this amazing question.

"Therefore speak unto them, and say unto them, Thus saith the Lord GOD; Every man of the house of Israel that setteth up his idols in his heart, and

39

putteth the stumbling block of his iniquity before his face, and cometh to the prophet; I the LORD will answer him that cometh *according to the multitude of his idols.*" (Ezekiel 14:4 KJV Italics added)

Idols are not just physical objects of worship. There are also idols of...

self-will

un-submissiveness

self-advancement

self-exultation

self-fill-in-the-blank.

A person with idolatry in his heart wants a word from God that feeds self-will. If it doesn't, then this inquirer will seek out another prophet and another word.

Un-submissiveness means that the person cares less about the government and the order of God because they have a rebellious heart.

The idolatrous inquirer serves God out of convenience only. Everything that could get in this person's way, that deals with the joys of this earth, keeps this person seperated from God. They are just interested in a bless-me-only God without any commitment.

```
┌─────────────────────────────────────┐
│                                       │
│       PROPHETIC DEFILEMENT            │
│       IS THE ASSIGNMENT USED          │
│       TO TAKE OUT THE PROPHET         │
│                                       │
└─────────────────────────────────────┘
```

As the rebellious inquirer comes before the prophet with all this idolatry in his heart God says, "I the Lord will answer him, and answer him according to the multitude of his idolatry." Wow! Let's look at the impact of this statement.

If a person approaches a prophet to inquire of the Lord who has idolatry in his heart of self-will and un-submissiveness, God is saying that He will answer him according to the idolatry in his heart. In other words, God will tell him what he wants to hear.

WHAT THEY WANT TO HEAR

A pastor told me that at his church they would have prophetic presbytery from time to time. A prophetic presbytery is where a prophetic team prophecies to each person that comes for prayer. However he told me that he did not want any more prophets speaking at the church. I asked him why. His response was, "Because every time these prophets prophesy over my people, they tell them just exactly what they want to hear. I know the people really well and they feed their rebellion and idolatry." That's it! Could it be that God was answering the people according to the idolatry in their hearts? Was he just telling them what they wanted to hear?

> "For everyone of the house of Israel, or of the stranger that sojourneth in Israel, which separateth himself from me, and setteth up his idols in his heart, and putteth the stumblingblock of his iniquity before his face, and cometh to a prophet to inquire of him concerning me; I the LORD will answer him by myself: {8} And I will set my face against that man, and will make him a sign and a proverb, and I will cut him off from the midst of my people; and ye shall know that I am the LORD." (Ezekiel 14:7-8 KJV)

From this verse we learn four important truths.

1. Idolatry separates you from God.

2. Idolatry is a stumbling block.

3. God opposes idols.

4. God will cut off the idolater.

To be cut off means that the prophet will be cut off from fresh revelation and new things that God is constantly bringing forth. Prophets need to be careful to renounce any idolatry of self-will, un-submission or self-advancement in their hearts.

Today many are approaching prophets requesting a personal prophecy. However some are approaching the prophets with idolatry and self-will in their hearts. They are not submissive to God or a local church. Some do not even go to church on a regular basis because of rebellion and a refusal to submit to any kind of spiritual oversight or covering. When they do, they gripe, complain, fuss, moan, and groan while doing nothing to help build the church.

I meet people like this at conferences. The prayer lines are full of them. Approaching the prophets for a prophetic word. You ask them, "Where do you go to church?" They say, "I don't go to church. I worship God in my own way." Or, "I can't find a church that I like." They say, "I don't like the pastor. I don't like this person or that person. The music is not very good. All they want is my money." I respond, "You are not called to like the pastors, you are called to love, respect, and support them and to help build that local church. There are lots of people that you may not like, yet you are required to love them."

True prophets are seeing through this idolatry and are saying, "You need to repent, get that idolatry out of your heart, and plug into a local church."

PROPHETIC PERMISSION

So what happens if a prophet prophesies to a person with idolatry in their hearts without God's permission? Is that prophet in sin?

"The prophet has not been granted permission to give an answer to the hypocritical inquirer but if the prophet does give the man the answer he desires [thus allowing himself to be a party to the inquirer's sin]. I the Lord will see to it that the prophet is deceived in his an-

> swer, and I will stretch out My
> hand against him and will de-
> stroy him from the midst of
> My people Israel." (Ezekiel 14:9
> AMP)

What? The prophet, who prophesies without permission will be deceived in his answer? What does this mean? It means that the prophet who gives the inquirer a personal prophecy that feeds idolatry, allows himself to be a party to the hypocritical inquirer's sin. Wow!

From this we learn why it is so important to have an unction (permission to speak) from the Holy Spirit before we prophesy. If the prophet does not have permission then God will stretch out his hand against the prophet and will destroy him too. *So we learn that the prophet who has not been granted permission to prophesy and yet does, is guilty of sin.*

PRESUMPTUOUS PROPHET

> "And they both shall bear the
> punishment of their iniquity:
> the iniquity of the [presumptu-
> ous] prophet shall be the same
> as the iniquity of the [hypocriti-
> cal] inquirer." (Ezekiel 14:10
> AMP)

45

Notice that scripture associates the prophet who prophesies without permission as presumptuous. A presumptuous prophet is one who thinks that God wants to speak all the time to people according to his faith alone and not according to the will of the Lord.

False prophecies, false prophetic operations, smooth sayings, people who prophesy out of their own spirit; or those who prophesy by the unction of Baal (divination) will release defilement upon themselves, and upon the people they prophesy to.

If we are to be a prophetic church, we need to guard ourselves against being defiled, feeding idolatry, or becoming partakers of another's sin. We must guard ourselves by being sure that we have permission (unction) from the Lord to prophesy (2 Peter 1:20,21). If we have permission then the burden falls upon the inquirer. If we do not have permission then we become partakers of the hypocritical inquirer's sin.

SUMMARY

☐All prophesy must be judged (1 John 4:1, 1 Corinthians 13:12).

☐Unction is permission of the Holy Spirit to prophesy (1 Peter 1:20-21).

☐Divination is trying to foretell the future by occult means.

☐The prophet who has not been granted permission to prophesy and yet does is guilty of sin (Ezekiel 14:9-10 AMP).

In the following chapter we will examine the prophetic operations of the prophet Balaam. In this prophet's life, we will see the result of an idolatrous heart, where demonic assignments pulled on the common ground that was in his heart.

Note
1 Jonas Clark, "Exposing Spiritual Witchcraft," (Hallandale, FL. Spirit of Life Publications, 1995)

48

CHAPTER 4

SEDUCING ASSIGNMENTS

Power, money, prestige, honor, promotion, and enticements with flattering smooth sayings are all demonic assignments designed to pull on any common ground that might be in the heart of God's prophetic ministers.

True prophetic operations must steer clear of money, honor, prestige, and promotion. These are all seducing assignments against God's true prophets. Let's look at how the Prophet Balaam fell prey to their enticements and was taken out.

The people of Moab were the children and the offspring of Lot and his daughter. They were an incestuous tribe. King Balak was terrified of the Israelites and was overcome with fear when he heard they were near. Balak, because of his fear, did not realize that the Israelites had already passed through his land, traveling from the south toward the north, and that he really had nothing to fear. The Israelites had already traveled on the king's highway and had passed the Moabites' territory.

TO BLESS OR CURSE

Acting out of fear King Balak sent messengers to God's prophet, Balaam, who lived in Pethor. Balaam was living 320 miles north of Moabite country near Haran. Abraham also lived in Haran, and you recall that Abraham left that heathen land at God's command to become the man that God called His friend.

> "Come now therefore, I pray thee, curse me this people; for they are too mighty for me: peradventure I shall prevail, that we may smite them, and that I may drive them out of the land: for I know that he whom thou blessest *is* blessed, and he whom thou cursest is cursed. {7} And the elders of Moab and the elders of Midian departed with the *rewards of divination* in their hand; and they came unto Balaam, and spake unto him the words of Balak." (Numbers 22:6-7 KJV Italics added)

Notice that these elders of Moab were sent with rewards in their hands, money for divination, and money for curses. They were prepared to buy the prophet's prophetic services. Were they known to be for sale?

> "And he (Balaam) said unto them, Lodge here this night, and I will bring you word again, as the Lord shall speak unto me: and the princes of Moab abode with Balaam." (Numbers 22:8 KJV)

Balaam asked these elders to spend the night that he might bring word as the Lord may speak. The word Lord here means Jehovah. If you have any wonder as to whom this prophet served, he was inquiring of Jehovah God. This would confirm that Balaam was a true prophet of God.

> "And God came unto Balaam, and said, What men are these with thee?" (Numbers 22:9 KJV)

God came to Balaam while he was praying and asked, "What men are these with you?" Do you think that God knew who these men were? The answer is obvious of

51

course. So then, God must have had a reason for asking Balaam who these men were. Let's read on.

> "And Balaam said unto God, Balak the son of Zippor, king of Moab, hath sent unto me, saying, {11} Behold, there is a people come out of Egypt, which covereth the face of the earth: come now, curse me them; peradventure I shall be able to overcome them, and drive them out. {12} And God said unto Balaam, *Thou shalt not go with them*; thou shalt not curse the people: for they are blessed." (Numbers 22:10-12 KJV Italics added)

Before we can go any further we must make something very clear. Did God say that Balaam could go with them? The answer is absolutely not. God said that he could not go and curse them because they were blessed. We need to make sure that we are all clear on this point because later God is going to let him go and we want to learn why.

> "And Balaam rose up in the morning, and said unto the

> princes of Balak, Get you into
> your land: for the Lord refuseth
> to give me leave to go with you."
> (Numbers 22:13 KJV)

The next morning Balaam told the princes of Balak to go back home because Jehovah refused to permit him to go with them. Isn't it interesting that Balaam did not tell the Moabites the rest of what God had told him? He failed to mention that they were blessed and could not be cursed by him.

> "And the princes of Moab rose
> up, and they went unto Balak,
> and said, Balaam refuseth to
> come with us." (Numbers 22:14
> KJV)

So the princes of Moab rose up and went back and told King Balak that Balaam the prophet refused to come with them. These princes did not tell the king the whole story either. They should have told the King that Jehovah God would not permit the prophet Balaam to come.

These communications got progressively worse by leaving the Word of the Lord out of the discussions. King Balak didn't know what was going on. He couldn't understand why the prophet wouldn't come. He thought that perhaps he hadn't offered him enough money. Now if the princes of Balak would have come back with the Word of the Lord saying, "Thou shalt not go. You can't curse them; they are blessed," then perhaps King Balak would have called off this whole thing.

FLATTERING PROMOTIONS

"And Balak sent yet again princes, more, and more honorable than they. {16} And they came to Balaam, and said to him, Thus saith Balak the son of Zippor, Let nothing, I pray thee, hinder thee from coming unto me: {17} For I will promote thee unto very great honor, and I will do whatsoever thou sayest unto me: come therefore, I pray thee, curse me this people." (Numbers 22:15-17 KJV)

"For I will promote thee." Can you see the p-u-l-l of these assignments against this prophet of God? Can you see the demonic enticements released against this prophet? Power, honor, money, prestige, enticements with smooth flattering sayings from the King's most honorable representatives. These are all high level demonic assignments designed to pull on any common ground that might be in the heart of God's prophet.

> "And Balaam answered and said unto the servants of Balak, If Balak would give me his house full of silver and gold, I cannot go beyond the word of the Lord my God, to do less or more." (Numbers 22:18)

Doesn't this sound honorable coming from the prophet Balaam? This is a good answer, yet he should also have reminded the delegation again what the Lord had said to him the first time. He should have said, "I don't know why you're wasting your time. God said that he would not permit me to go and to curse them, for they have already been blessed." Let's read what the prophet does.

> "Now therefore, I pray you, tarry ye also here this night, that I may know what the Lord will say unto me more." (Numbers 22:19 KJV)

This was Balaam's second mistake. God had already spoken to him saying, "Thou shalt not go with them; you shall not curse the people, for they are blessed." Yet Balaam is going to speak with God about it again.

> "And God came unto Balaam at night, and said unto him, If the men come to call thee, rise up, and go with them; but yet the word which I shall say unto thee, that shalt thou do." (Numbers 22:20 KJV)

Did God change His mind? Why would God tell Balaam not to go and then tell him to go? Was God answering Balaam according to the idolatry in his heart?

Is it dangerous to keep pressing God in prayer after he has already spoken? Were these demonic assignments still seeking common ground in Balaam's heart? Why did God change his mind?

DOES GOD CHANGE HIS MIND?

I see this happen many times. People come to me and say, "Apostle, I have prayed about this and God said that I need to do such and such." I look at them and say, "You prayed about this and you are sure that you have heard from God?" They say, "Yes, I am quite sure." Three or four months pass by, and then they say, "Well Apostle, it's not working out — God must have changed his mind."

THE PROPHET WHO HAS NOT BEEN GRANTED PERMISSION TO PROPHESY AND YET DOES, IS GUILTY OF SIN

Do you know what I am talking about? Perhaps this has happened to you too. You thought that God had said for you to do something and then all of a sudden it seemed like God changed his mind. Be honest now, you just knew that God had spoken to you. You knew it was God but now it looks like he changed his mind. What happened? Something went wrong, right? Either you did not hear God right the first time or something went terribly wrong. Am I right? Was it God, or wasn't it God? Some walk around saying that it was God who spoke, but then are not sure and later on say, "I guess God changed his mind."

Again, what did God say to Balaam? He said, "Thou shalt not go." Now Balaam inquired again of the Lord and God told him then to go. Why did God change his mind? Again let's look for the answer in the prophetic life of Ezekiel.

> "Son of man, these men have
> set up their idols in their heart,
> and put the stumblingblock of
> their iniquity before their face:
> should I be inquired of at all by
> them?" (Ezekiel 14:3 KJV)

What does it mean to put the "stumbling block of their iniquity before their faces?" Stumbling blocks are those things in our lives that are more important to us than God. They are idols. These men who approached Ezekiel were asking God to bless their idols.

Balaam had it in his heart to go. He continued to press God for permission even after God had told him not to go. Balaam could be bought. The demonic assignment was working. The hook was set. The prey captured. Balaam was crossing the threshold.

BLESS MY IDOLS

Idols are very dangerous. God severally opposes anything that separates him from his children. Idols are anything that separate you from God. If God asked you to do something for him, but there was always something else that you had to do first, then that could be idolatry. Whatever it is that consistently pulls you away from the Father is idolatry. The real insult to God is when one asks God to bless their stumbling blocks of idolatry.

Modern man may not bow down to wooden idols yet there are many other idols. Idolatry is anything that pulls you away from God. Idols might be a man, woman, job, house, car, children, money, television, sports, hobbies, animals or even your ministry. Whatever it is that separates your heart from an intimate relationship with Jesus, is idolatry. Idols can represent things in your heart that the enemy can use to pull on you, like idols of self-will. Some say "God blesses the work of your hands," but if the work of your hands pulls you away from God, it is not the blessings from God.

The demonic enticements against Balaam were designed to find any idols in his heart that the enemy could use to separate him from God. Prophets must guard themselves against these same demonic assignments.

> "Therefore speak unto them, and say unto them, Thus saith the Lord GOD; Every man of the house of Israel that setteth up his idols in his heart, and putteth the stumbling block of his iniquity before his face, and cometh to the prophet; *I the Lord will answer him that*

cometh according to the multitude of his idols." (Ezekiel 14:4 KJV Italics added)

There are many people asking God to bless their idolatry even after God has already said no. But because of their persistence there is a danger that God will answer them according to the multitudes of their idolatry. In other words, it may appear that God seems to be changing his mind by telling them only what they really want to hear. The solid balance for direction of any servant of God is his written word. The Holy Spirit will never violate what's already been written.

BALAAM'S IDOLATRY

Let's look again at what the prophet Balaam did. Remember God clearly said, "Thou shalt not go," then he told Balaam to go.

"And God came unto Balaam at night, and said unto him, If the men come to call thee, rise up, and go with them; but yet the word which I shall say unto thee, that shalt thou do." (Numbers 22:20 KJV)

God looks at our heart to see what is in there (Psalm 7:9). Balaam was ready and anxious to go with the Moabites. God had spoken to Balaam saying that he could not go. Did God change his mind? Not really, but God tested the prophet to see what was in his heart. With God's permission Balaam saddled up his donkey and set out for Moab country.

> "And God's anger was kindled because he went: and the angel of the Lord stood in the way for an adversary against him. Now he was riding upon his ass, and his two servants were with him."
> (Numbers 22:22 KJV)

God's anger was kindled against Balaam. Some are asking, "But God, you said that he could go." True, but that did not mean that Balaam was supposed to go. Can you see this? God had answered Balaam according to the idolatry in his heart because Balaam had continued to press God in prayer.

God may do that to us too. God might say, "Well, if you really want to do that, even after I have already said no, then go ahead." You had better watch out though, you could be entering a test. Some people call me and ask me, "Where is that scripture that says that God will give you the desires of your

61

heart?" I tell them, "Right here!" (Ezekiel 14:4). God will give you the desires of your heart to prove and to test you, but what if the desires of your heart are not right? It is always important that we examine our motives.

BALAAM'S ANGRY HEART

God's anger was kindled against the prophet Balaam "because he went."

> "And the ass saw the angel of the Lord standing in the way, and his sword drawn in his hand: and the ass turned aside out of the way, and went into the field: and Balaam smote the ass, to turn her into the way. {24} But the angel of the Lord stood in a path of the vineyards, a wall being on this side, and a wall on that side. {25} And when the ass saw the angel of the Lord, she thrust herself unto the wall, and crushed Balaam's foot against the wall: and he smote her again. {26} And the angel of the Lord went further, and stood in a narrow place, where was no way to turn either to the right hand or to the

left. {27} And when the ass saw the angel of the Lord, she fell down under Balaam: and Balaam's anger was kindled, and he smote the ass with a staff." (Numbers 22:23-27)

Balaam's anger was kindled because he was being delayed and he struck his donkey. Notice the anger in the prophet's heart? Nothing was going to get in Balaam's way. Nothing was going to stop him from his pursuit, not even a faithful donkey.

"And the Lord opened the mouth of the ass, and she said unto Balaam, What have I done unto thee, that thou hast smitten me these three times? {29} And Balaam said unto the ass, Because thou hast mocked me: I would there were a sword in mine hand, for now would I kill thee." (Numbers 22:28-29 KJV)

The way Balaam responded to his animal revealed a deep-seated anger in his life. He was full of murder and self-will. A murderous, self-will spirit was in the heart of this prophet. Nothing would keep him from the idolatry in his heart. He was even ready to kill his own faithful donkey. Anger and murder rose up in his heart to defend his idolatry. God was testing Balaam's heart to see what was in it and he was failing miserably.

God was angry with Balaam because he had told him not to go and yet he went anyway. Why did Balaam want to go? Because he had been enticed by the rewards for divination. These demonic assignments had found common ground in Balaam's heart.

> "And the ass said unto Balaam, Am not I thine ass, upon which thou hast ridden ever since I was thine unto this day? was I ever wont to do so unto thee? And he said, Nay. {31} Then the Lord opened the eyes of Balaam, and he saw the angel of the Lord standing in the way, and his sword drawn in his hand: and he bowed down his head, and fell flat on his face. {32} And the angel of the Lord said unto him, Wherefore hast thou smitten thine ass these three times? behold, I went out to withstand thee, because *thy way is perverse before me*:" (Numbers 22:30-32 KJV Italics added)

The word perverse means to deviate from what is considered right. The angel was saying, "I know that I told you that you could go, but your behavior is contrary, it's obstinate. You're not walking according to my ways. You have taken the wrong course." Balaam's idolatry was being exposed. He was unreasonably determined to have his own way.

To have one's own way is the idolatry of self-will. Balaam the prophet wanted the "rewards of divination." He wanted all that King Balak had offered him...

fame

money

honor

power

prestige

promotion.

What was in Balaam's heart that would have him even murder his own donkey? It was idolatry and God was exposing it.

Balaam was a true prophet of God who was deceived and enticed by witchcraft. He was pulled away from the Word of God by the common ground of idolatry and self-will that was in his own heart. All the divination and the enticements by King Balak were released at him and he took it into the common ground of his heart. Balaam was probably thinking, "I can be somebody. All I have to do is go curse these people. After all, what's the big deal? A few little prophetic curses and I am out of there. This is my big chance for promotion."

BABYLONIAN DIVINATION

Now let's continue and see how Balaam got off into prophetic error.

> "And the angel of the Lord said unto Balaam, Go with the men: but only the word that I shall speak unto thee, that thou shalt speak. So Balaam went with the princes of Balak." (Numbers 22:35 KJV)

Again, Balaam could have stopped right here, instead of going with the princes of Balak. He could have said, "Lord, forgive me, I heard you the first time and I am going back." God gave Balaam another chance because he was still proving the prophet's heart.

"And it came to pass on the morrow, that Balak took Balaam, and brought him up into the high places of Baal, that thence he might see the utmost part of the people." (Numbers 22:41 KJV)

"And Balaam said unto Balak, Build me here seven altars, and prepare me here seven oxen and seven rams." (Numbers 23:1 KJV)

This is the working of Babylonian divination. Balaam was from Pethor that was in the land of Abraham's father called the land of Ur of the Chaldees. This was the heartland of pagan divination and witchcraft in those days. Balaam had seen the practices of Babylonian divination and he knew what would be impressive to King Balak. God never told Balaam to build these seven altars and prepare these oxen and rams; that was Babylonian divination.

Balaam had no intention of seeking God for a revelation or a prophetic word. He wanted to impress the king and pickup his rewards. Those altars were the Babylonian way of conjuring up demons through divination and occult practice.

Divination means to tap into the "divine" through sorcery. It is the act or practice of trying to foretell the future by occult means.

> "And Balak did as Balaam had spoken; and Balak and Balaam offered on every altar a bullock and a ram. 3 And Balaam said unto Balak, Stand by thy burnt offering, and I will go: *peradventure* (perhaps) the Lord will come to meet me: and whatsoever he showeth me I will tell thee. And he went to an high place. {4} And God met Balaam: and he said unto him, I have prepared seven altars, and I have offered upon every altar a bullock and a ram. {5} And the Lord put a word in Balaam's mouth, and said, Return unto Balak, and thus thou shalt speak." (Numbers 23:2-5 KJV Italics added)

Balaam said *"perhaps"* the Lord will speak to me, but Balaam never had it in his heart to talk to or inquire of the Lord. If he had, he would not have said, "Perhaps," He would have said, "God is going to speak to me because I am here on an assignment and God said go and speak what I tell you." Did

Balaam do that? No! Balaam did not go aside to get a prophetic word from the Lord, but to Balaam's surprise God did speak. God did put some words in his mouth. All the while testing this old prophet's heart. Can you see that? So Balaam came back and spoke blessings over Israel.

> "And he returned unto him, and, lo, he stood by his burnt sacrifice, he, and all the princes of Moab. {7} And he took up his parable, and said, Balak the king of Moab hath brought me from Aram, out of the mountains of the east, saying, Come, curse me Jacob, and come, defy Israel. {8} How shall I curse, whom God hath not cursed? or how shall I defy, whom the Lord hath not defied? {9} For from the top of the rocks I see him, and from the hills I behold him: lo, the people shall dwell alone, and shall not be reckoned among the nations. {10} Who can count the dust of Jacob, and the number of the fourth part of Israel? Let me die the death of the righteous, and let my last end be like his!" (Numbers 23:6-10 KJV)

"And Balak said unto Balaam,
What hast thou done unto me?
I took thee to curse mine enemies, and, behold, thou hast
blessed them altogether. {12}
And he answered and said,
Must I not take heed to speak
that which the Lord hath put
in my mouth?" (Numbers
23:11-12 KJV)

King Balak was so upset. He had brought
the prophet Balaam to curse Israel and
Balaam had blessed them. I think this even
surprised Balaam. Balaam wanted the
money; he wanted the wages of divination.
He couldn't believe himself what was coming out of his mouth. So then he began to
defend himself and say, "Didn't I tell you
whatever God said, that I would have to
speak?" This was all a defense to keep himself from being killed by King Balak.

"Surely there is no enchantment
against Jacob, neither is there
any divination against Israel: according to this time it shall be
said of Jacob and of Israel, What
hath God wrought!" (Numbers
23:23 KJV)

Balaam had been trying to curse the Israelites by tapping into a spirit of divination to release these curses, but he realized
that it couldn't be done and he told King
Balak, "There is no divination or witchcraft
that will curse Israel." God all along the way
was proving, trying, and testing the idolatry in the heart of his prophet, Balaam, in
an effort to reach him.

DIVINATION AND SEXUAL SIN

> "And Israel abode in Shittim,
> and the people began to com-
> mit whoredom with the daugh-
> ters of Moab." (Numbers 25:1
> KJV)

Balaam concluded that it was impossible
to curse Israel by divination, yet he had
crossed over the threshold through his idolatry and rebellion because he still wanted his
rewards for divination. So, he instructed
King Balak in the way that would corrupt
Israel. Balaam told King Balak to corrupt
the tribes with whoredoms with the daughters of Moab.

"We can't get them this way, God won't
let us curse them so send the women into
their camp; have them entice the men to
come and worship with them in the their
pagan high places. Send the daughters of

Moab into the camp and that will bring defilement upon the Israelites and take them out from under the protective covering of God. Tell the women to have sex with them, have them partake of your love feast and then you will have them."

GOD'S PROPHETS MUST AVOID THE SPIRIT OF BALAAM AT ALL COST

This was Balaam's sin and it all started because of the idolatry in his own heart. *Divination always releases sexual sins.* That is what Balaam did. Balaam knew that he could entice the men of God through lust. All the armies of the enemies of the Israelites could not defeat them but they could be defiled through the lust of the flesh.

THE GREAT SIN OF BALAAM

The great sin of Balaam was not only the merchandising of his anointing and the attempt at cursing Israel, rather it was teaching the Moabites how to *defile* God's people. Balaam knew the word of God forbade the intermingling of God's people with foreign women (Deuteronomy 7:1-4). He knew that introducing whoredoms would cause the Israelites to break covenant with God.

The word whoredom is the Hebrew word *zanah*, meaning to go a whoring, commit fornication or adultery. By targeting Israel with the Moabite whoredoms, he ushered in Babylonian paganism and foreign gods. This unholy mixture was a demonic assignment designed to...

> turn the people from the word of God

> break the covenant between God and Israel

> defile the blood line and keep the Messiah (Jesus) from being able to be born.

God's prophets must avoid the spirit of Balaam at all cost. Because of this great evil, God terminated Balaam's ministry and his life. He will forever be remembered as a traitor.

> "Behold, these caused the children of Israel, through the counsel of Balaam, to commit trespass against the Lord in the matter of Peor, and there was a

plague among the congregation of the Lord." (Numbers 31:16 KJV)

God broke out against the Israelites who went for the women and killed them by plague. God instructed Moses to avenge the Israelites on the Midianites and they slew every male including the prophet Balaam. What a sad truth to learn that Balaam, once a true prophet of God, could be enticed by the idolatry in his own heart to sin against God. Idolatry must be avoided at all cost.

SUMMARY

☐True prophetic operations must steer clear of money, honor, prestige, and promotion. These are all high level demonic assignments designed to pull on any common ground that might be in the heart of God's prophet.

☐Stumbling blocks are those things in our lives that are more important to us than God.

☐Modern man may not bow down to wooden idols yet there

are many other idols. Idolatry is anything that pulls you away from God.

☐Divination means to tap into the "divine" through sorcery. It is the act or practice of trying to foretell the future by occult means.

☐Divination always releases sexual sins.

☐The great sin of Balaam was not only the merchandising of his anointing and the attempt at cursing Israel, rather it was teaching the Moabites how to defile God's people.

Next we will look at an unliked prophet whom God used to speak to a king.

CHAPTER 5

THE UNLIKED PROPHET

The prophetic ministry is not always liked or received. Oftentimes it even violates public opinion. Micaiah is a great example of God preparing a prophet to speak to a coveting King.

L et's take a look at another example where God answers someone according to the idolatry in his heart. It's the story of when King Ahab met Micaiah, God's prophet.

Ahab was the wicked King who married Jezebel. Jezebel so hated the prophets of God that she had thousands of them murdered or driven into caves for fear of losing their lives. Ahab, allowing these murders to take place, himself did more to provoke God than all the kings before him.

> "And they continued three years without war between Syria and Israel. {2} And it came to pass in the third year, that

Jehoshaphat the king of Judah
came down to the king of Israel.
{3} And the king of Israel said
unto his servants, Know ye that
Ramoth in Gilead is ours, and
we be still, and take it not out
of the hand of the king of Syria?"
(1 Kings 22:1-3 KJV)

Syria and Israel were at peace with one
another. King Ahab of Israel revealed the
covetousness in his heart when he told King
Jehoshaphat of Judah; "Everything the king
of Syria has is ours for the taking."

"And Jehoshaphat said unto
the king of Israel, Inquire, I pray
thee, at the word of the Lord
today. {6} Then the king of Israel gathered the prophets together, about four hundred
men, and said unto them, Shall
I go against Ramothgilead to
battle, or shall I forbear? And
they said, Go up; for the Lord
shall deliver it into the hand of
the king." (1 Kings 22:5-6 KJV)

GO UP AND TAKE IT

Let's look in the heart of King Ahab.
"Know ye that Ramoth in Gilead is ours?"
Jehoshaphat, King of Judah was not con-
78

vinced so he asked for a prophetic inquiry. In response King Ahab gathered four hundred prophets (pride) to inquire of the Lord on behalf of King Jehoshaphat to put his unease and concern to rest.

So the prophets responded to the king's prophetic inquiry by saying, "Go up and conquer it, no problem, for the Lord shall deliver it into the hand of the king." Four hundred prophets were prophesying the same thing. Can you imagine?

> "And Jehoshaphat said, Is there not here a prophet of the Lord besides, that we might inquire of him?" (1 Kings 22:7 KJV)

Jehoshaphat sensed that something was not quite right with these prophets and he asked for yet another. Now Ahab was going to inquire of four hundred and one prophets. You would think that four hundred prophets would have been enough but there was something that prompted this king to ask for another prophet. God will always send, "His Word." He will always get His Word through.

THE UNLIKED PROPHET

> "And the king of Israel said unto Jehoshaphat, There is yet one

man, Micaiah the son of Imlah,
by whom we may inquire of the
Lord: *but I hate him; for he doth
not prophesy good concerning
me,* but evil. And Jehoshaphat
said, Let not the king say so."
(1 Kings 22:8 KJV Italics added)

Ahab said there was one more prophet
that was not present named Micaiah, but
King Ahab hated him. Every time he inquired of that prophet he prophesied evil
things. King Ahab didn't like it; there was
hatred in his heart because Micaiah never
prophesied anything good to him. There were
no smooth sayings in his mouth. Every time
King Ahab talked to this prophet, he exposed sin in his heart. He hated him.
Micaiah was the unliked prophet. I can almost hear King Ahab talking to himself, "Do
we have to call him? He's the only prophet
not here, but I don't like him. He always
has something bad to say. He makes me
nervous."

I think King Ahab had a little experience with this prophet Micaiah. What do
you think? Some of you may not know this,
but Ahab many times had his hands full
dealing with yet another prophet named
Elijah who once told Ahab there would be

no rain unless he said so (1 Kings 17). God had two national prophets available to speak to King Ahab.

> "Then the king of Israel called an officer, and said, Hasten hither Micaiah the son of Imlah. {10} And the king of Israel and Jehoshaphat the king of Judah sat each on his throne, having put on their robes, in a void place in the entrance of the gate of Samaria; and all the prophets prophesied before them." (1 Kings 22:9-10 KJV)

King Ahab sent for Micaiah the prophet. While they waited at the city gate the four hundred prophets stood before the kings where one after another prophesied only of good things. They were prophesying smooth sayings. Did God give these prophets an unction to prophesy? Because he did not, witchcraft, confusion, and prophetic defilement were being released by them. Had they tapped into the Spirit of God with their inquiries, or had they tapped into a spirit of divination?

> "And Zedekiah the son of Chenaanah made him horns of iron: and he said, Thus saith

> the Lord, With these shalt thou
> push the Syrians, until thou
> have consumed them." (1 Kings
> 22:11 KJV)

In the midst of this prophetic gathering rose a prophet named Zedekiah boldly saying, "Thus saith the Lord." He got everyone's attention as he stepped forward. Zedekiah the prophet stood up with horns of iron grasped firmly in his hands being used as prophetic symbols said, "With these you shall push the Syrians until they are destroyed." He was delivering a prophetic word. Everybody stopped and listened intently including the other three hundred ninety-nine prophets and both kings. It seemed like Zedekiah was speaking as one with authority.

> "And all the prophets proph-
> esied so, saying, Go up to Ra-
> mothgilead, and prosper: for the
> Lord shall deliver it into the
> king's hand." (1 Kings 22:12
> KJV)

Everyone heard Zedekiah prophesy and all the prophets got into agreement with him. They were probably saying things like, "That witnesses with me. Yeah, I got a witness to that too. It must be God. That's the well known Zedekiah, of course I got a witness to that." Does any of this sound familiar? Nothing seems to change. Everyone agreed saying, "Go up and prosper." Three hundred and ninety-nine other prophets agreed with Zedekiah's false prophetic operation. Public opinion was set.

SMOOTH SAYINGS

"And the messenger that was gone to call Micaiah spake unto him, saying, Behold now, the words of the prophets declare good unto the king with one mouth: let thy word, I pray thee, be like the word of one of them, and speak that which is good." (1 Kings 22:13 KJV)

King Ahab sent a messenger to get the unliked prophet, Micaiah. After finding him this messenger told Micaiah what was going on and that the other prophets had already spoken. He told him, "Everyone else has already spoken on behalf of God with a good word, so why don't you? Let's all get into agreement. Can't we all just get along? We don't want division around here or anything like that, you know. We all got a witness to it too, brother."

> "And Micaiah said, As the Lord
> liveth, what the Lord saith unto
> me, that will I speak." (1 Kings
> 22:14 KJV)

Let's just make sure that we understand what Micaiah, God's prophet, just said. Again he said, "As the Lord lives, I will speak what the Lord says." Now let's read what the Lord said. God is about to use Micaiah to answer Ahab's inquiry according to the idolatry in his heart. He is going to tell him what he wants to hear. Are you ready for this?

POPULAR PROPHETIC OPINION

> "So he came to the king. And
> the king said unto him, Mica-
> iah, shall we go against Ra-
> mothgilead to battle, or shall we
> forbear? And he answered him,
> Go, and prosper: for the Lord
> shall deliver it into the hand of
> the king." (1 Kings 22:15 KJV)

Now, everyone who is confused read intently. What in the world is going on? What was it that Micaiah said? He said, "Whatever the Lord says, that will I speak." Now what was it that the Lord spoke through

Micaiah the prophet? "Go and prosper for the Lord shall deliver it into the hand of the king." Again we see God answer someone according to the idolatry in their heart. King Ahab had put the stumbling block of his iniquity before the prophet (Ezekiel 14:3). Micaiah just agreed with the other four hundred prophets! Can you imagine? But watch what happened next.

> "And the king said unto him, How many times shall I adjure thee that thou tell me nothing but that which is true in the name of the Lord?" (1 Kings 22:16 KJV)

Micaiah had prophesied so many contrary things to King Ahab, that even King Ahab does not believe his own ears. Ahab was saying in his heart, "This can't be right. How can this prophet be so agreeable with popular prophetic opinion when I know that he never is?" Even Ahab was wise enough to know that something was not right. Micaiah then began to speak the true "Word of the Lord." Watch this.

> "And he said, I saw all Israel scattered upon the hills, as sheep that have not a shepherd: and the Lord said, These have

no master: let them return every man to his house in peace."
(1 Kings 22:17 KJV)

Does this prophetic utterance say that all will go well with the king? No! Let's continue.

> "And the king of Israel said unto Jehoshaphat, Did I not tell thee that he would prophesy no good concerning me, but evil? {19} And he said, Hear thou therefore the word of the Lord: I saw the Lord sitting on his throne, and all the host of heaven standing by him on his right hand and on his left." (1 Kings 22:18-19 KJV)

Unlike the prophet Balaam, Micaiah is not motivated by anyone but Jehovah God himself. Being popular among the other prophets is not in his heart. Here we see a true prophetic operation. *All prophets must guard their hearts from the potential control of being liked by the public.*

King Ahab had idolatry in his heart. He wanted to conquer Syria and he would do it at any cost.

A LYING SPIRIT

Micaiah first answered Ahab according to his idolatry but by God's mercy and grace released a true prophetic utterance. Would Ahab have ears to hear? Or was his idolatry and covetousness going to get him killed?

Let's take a look behind the scenes at this prophetic gathering before the two kings.

> "And the Lord said, Who shall persuade Ahab, that he may go up and fall at Ramothgilead? And one said on this manner, and another said on that manner. *{21}* And there came forth a spirit, and stood before the Lord, and said, I will persuade him. *{22}* And the Lord said unto him, Wherewith? And he said, I will go forth, and I will be a *lying spirit in the mouth of all his prophets.* And he said, Thou shalt persuade him, and prevail also: go forth, and do so." (1 Kings 22:20-22 KJV Italics added)

In other words, God permitted a lying spirit, to speak because King Ahab had idolatry, self-will, and covetousness in his heart. God was going to answer Ahab according to the idolatry in his heart.

> "Now therefore, behold, the Lord hath put a lying spirit in the mouth of all these thy prophets, and the Lord hath spoken evil concerning thee. {24} But Zedekiah the son of Chenaanah went near, and smote Micaiah on the cheek, and said, Which way went the spirit of the Lord from me to speak unto thee?" (1 Kings 22:23-24 KJV)

Zedekiah slaps Micaiah on his cheek and asks, "How is it possible that the Holy Spirit stopped using me and began to use you?" Prophetic error releases a spirit of pride. Zedekiah thought that he had put the amen on the prophetic conference. How dare Micaiah do something contrary.

A lying spirit seeks to mock the true prophetic voice of God, and reading the rest of this chapter will tell the story of Ahab's battle as his forces were defeated and himself mortally wounded (1 Kings 22:37). Self-will, idolatry, and covetousness got Ahab killed. I often wonder if Zedekiah and the other prophets were ever held accountable for missing it. Ahab is a great example of carnal living.

SUMMARY

☐The prophet's ministry is not always liked or received. Oftentimes it even violates public opinion.

☐God used Micaiah to answer King Ahab according to the idolatry in his heart.

☐Prophets must guard their hearts from the potential control of being liked by the public.

☐Self-will, idolatry and covetousness got Ahab killed.

In the next chapter we will discover the power of prophetic words. Spoken prophetic declarations out of the prophet's mouth can release prophetic defilement if he flows prophetically outside of the unction of the Holy Spirit.

CHAPTER 6

POWER IN PROPHETIC WORDS

The prophetic tongue that is not flowing through an accurate prophetic operation can release iniquity, lawlessness, and prophetic defilement. However, prophets who are flowing accurately can bring great blessing to the body of Christ. God uses prophets to announce, activate, impart, confirm, and unlock times and seasons.

Life and death are in the power of the tongue (Proverbs 18:21). Yet there has been resistance to the understanding of what happens when prophetic words are spoken outside of the unction of the Holy Spirit. Let's just take everyday conversation for an example of the power of words. If I were to tell you that you looked great today then that probably would make you feel better about yourself. If I asked, "What happened to you?" And said, "You look awful." That would probably make you feel uneasy about your appearance. So we learn that natural words cause an effect. How much more that of prophetic words?

Prophetic operations have a powerful effect in the realm of the Spirit. Words give life and credibility to what comes out of the heart. They give a spiritual measure to what is spoken. Prophetic words are powerful! Because of their power, prophets need to be careful to flow in accurate operations. I am convinced that defilement is a major weapon used to destroy the prophet's ministry. Jesus speaks of defilement when he says it is, "Not that which goeth into the mouth defileth a man; but that which cometh out of the mouth, this defileth a man" (Matthew 15:11 KJV).

Throughout the church there has been a release of defilement in the land by false prophetic operations. God always counteracts these things with true prophetic operations. It is important to understand that God does not want his prophets defiled. God wants prophetic operations to be pure, holy, and accurate in his sight. Holiness and right living is a guard against defilement.

> "But as he which hath called
> you is holy, so be ye holy in all
> manner of conversation; {16}
> Because it is written, Be ye holy;
> for I am holy." (1 Peter 1:15-16
> KJV)

Jesus taught his disciples that what goes into the mouth does not defile the man, but what comes out of the mouth that can defile the man. Spoken prophetic words out of the prophet's mouth can release a spiritual defilement if he prophesies outside of the unction (permission) of the Spirit. When Jesus spoke of this defilement that can come out of a person's mouth he offended the Pharisees.

> "Then came his disciples, and said unto him, Knowest thou that the Pharisees were offended, after they heard this saying? {13} But he answered and said, Every plant, which my heavenly Father hath not planted, shall be rooted up. {14} Let them alone: they be blind leaders of the blind. And if the blind lead the blind, both shall fall into the ditch." (Matthew 15:12-14 KJV)

Notice that the Pharisees, the religious legalist, were offended when hearing about this defilement. We need to understand that truth will offend the Pharisees every time. These legalist are still around today. They carry a critical, religious, letter of the law spirit.

93

The Pharisees will always challenge deep spiritual truth that deals with the issues of a man's heart. They can't see past the natural and gaze into the spiritual because they are carnally minded, not spiritually minded.

True prophetic operations speak the truth in love without trying to defend God. They leave the Pharisees to debate one another. *Religion loves debate.* Prophets are not sent to debate the Word of God, they are sent to speak the Word of God. The Pharisees are blind leaders of the blind who can't be helped. Prophets today should not set their eyes on the Pharisees because they will never understand true prophetic operations. In fact, their desire is to crucify or at best quiet the prophets.

SPIRITUAL DISCERNMENT

Prophetic words and spiritual discernment go together. Spiritual discernment is the ability to separate the true from the false. Further it means to have a spiritual understanding that does not come about through intellect or reasoning. *The prophetic gift is the most spiritually discerning of all the fivefold ministry gifts.*

"Then answered Peter and said unto him, Declare unto us this parable. {16} And Jesus said,

Are ye also yet without understanding? {17} Do not ye yet
understand, that whatsoever
entereth in at the mouth goeth
into the belly, and is cast out
into the draught? {18} But those
things which proceed out of the
mouth come forth from the
heart; and they defile the man.
{19} For out of the heart proceed evil thoughts, murders,
adulteries, fornications, thefts,
false witness, blasphemies: {20}
These are the things which defile a man: but to eat with un-
washen hands defileth not a
man." (Matthew 15:15-20 KJV)

Peter asked the Lord to explain this parable of defilement to him. Let's look at what
Jesus said. "Are you also still without understanding?" In other words, are you operating without spiritual discernment? Sometimes it is hard to understand why these
men who spent so much time with the Lord
did not grasp the depth of this teaching.
The reality was that this parable must be
spiritually discerned. The disciples could not
just understand it with their heads. They
had to get its meaning by the Holy Spirit.

Through this parable we also understand that those things that proceed out of the prophetic mouth through the heart, come from our innermost being. They come out of our spirits and if we are flowing accurately, then they will come by the Spirit himself into and through our spirit.

Not only can prophetic words give life, direction, warning, and release blessing, they can also defile us if we have not received permission by the Spirit of God to prophesy. The prophet must, above all, guard his heart and his tongue.

TIMES AND SEASONS

Prophets who are flowing accurately can bring great blessing to the body of Christ. God uses prophets to...

announce

activate

impart

confirm

unlock.

Prophets open doors to various times and seasons in one's life. Every new thing, new door of opportunity, or advancement in my ministry was first announced or confirmed by a prophetic operation.

> **ALL PROPHETS MUST GUARD THEIR HEARTS FROM THE POTENTIAL CONTROL OF BEING LIKED BY THE PUBLIC**

The prophetic tongue has the ability to bless or defile. There are natural seasons and there are spiritual seasons. There is natural timing and there is spiritual timing. The prophetic tongue can set on fire the very course of nature, or unlock times and seasons in our lives.

As I have traveled throughout the world preaching the gospel I notice an intense frustration in the hearts of God's people. I believe that frustration is because believers know that the gift inside of them is much larger than what they currently see in their lives. This is an indication of the importance of the prophetic ministry gifts who throughout the word of God, are used to announce and unlock the next season in one's life. When we understand the prophets role in activating and confirming then we can benefit from his gifting.

97

The good news is that accurate prophetic operations can unlock your destiny. The Lord does nothing without revealing it first to his prophets (Amos 3:7).

Let's look at several prophetic operations that released individuals into a new time and season in their lives.

PROPHETIC ANNOUNCEMENTS

To announce means to make known by formal notice. The following are examples of prophetic announcements that unlocked times and seasons in another's life. We too can expect to see spiritual seasons prophetically announced and unlocked to us.

ANGEL OF THE LORD TO MARY (LUKE 1:28-33)

One of the most well known prophetic announcements was to Mary when the angel of the Lord told her that she was highly favored and would bring forth a son named Jesus who would be the Savior of the world. This announcement changed Mary's life forever. It opened the door for a new season in her life.

JOHN THE BAPTIST OF THE LORD (JOHN 1:29)

John the Baptist made a prophetic announcement when he declared, "Behold the

Lamb of God, which taketh away the sin of the world." John the Baptist was the fore-runner of Christ ministry. From this we learn that even in Jesus' ministry there was a prophetic announcement. This prophetic announcement revealed a new season in our Lord's ministry.

SAMUEL TO DAVID (1 SAMUEL 16)

Samuel made a prophetic announce-ment and impartation when he took a horn of oil and anointed David in the midst of his brethren. When he did so the Spirit of the Lord came upon David from that day forward. God unlocked a new season in his life through a prophetic operation.

THE ANGEL TO GIDEON (JUDGES 6:12)

The angel of the Lord made a prophetic announcement to Gideon when he said, "Go in this thy might, and thou shalt save Israel from the hand of the Midianites: have not I sent thee?" Prior to this prophetic release Gideon had seen himself as the least in his father's house. This prophetic announce-ment stirred faith and action for a new day in Gideon's heart. The announcement un-locked a new season in Gideon's life.

GOD TO MOSES (EXODUS 4)

One day Moses climbed the mountain to see the great sight of the burning bush. The Lord spoke to him and told him that he had heard the cry of the children of Israel because of their great oppression. Then God prophetically announced to Moses his ministry of deliverance, "Come now therefore, and I will send thee unto Pharaoh, that thou mayest bring forth my people the children of Israel out of Egypt" (Exodus 4:10). Moses was impacted mightily by this prophetic decree. A new season had been unlocked to him.

JOSEPH'S PROPHETIC DREAM (GENESIS 37:6-10)

Joseph received a prophetic dream that announced a coming dominion authority. This prophetic dream so angered his brothers that they sought means to kill him and they sold him into slavery.

PAUL & BARNABAS (ACTS 13:3)

The Antioch church's presbytery made a prophetic announcement by the unction of the Holy Spirit as they were ministering to the Lord and fasting when he said, "Separate me Barnabas and Saul for the work whereunto I have called them." Then they

100

laid their hands on them and sent them (*apo-stello*) away. The prophetic announcement opened the door for a new season in Barnabas and Saul's ministry.

CONFIRMATION IMPARTATION & ACTIVATION

Not only does the prophetic gift deliver prophetic announcements it also provides confirmation, impartation and activation.

MOSES & JOSHUA (DEUTERONOMY 34:9)

Moses transferred the spirit of wisdom to Joshua when he laid his hands on him. This prophetic impartation activated Joshua in a greater spiritual capacity.

TIMOTHY & PRESBYTERY (1 TIMOTHY 4:14)

Timothy received the Holy Spirit and an activation in ministry through a prophetic presbytery.

PAUL & ANANIAS (ACTS 9:17)

The Apostle Paul himself received an impartation and activation into ministry when the prophet Ananias laid his hands on him.

It was through the prophetic ministry of Ananias that we see Paul being confirmed and activated into ministry.

ELIJAH & ELISHA (2 KINGS 2:13)

When Elijah was taken up into heaven he threw down his mantel and Elisha grabbed it and struck the waters with it. The prophets acknowledged that the spirit of Elijah then rested on Elisha and they came to meet him and bowed themselves to the ground before him. Elisha's ministry was then confirmed and activated. A new season was unlocked to him.

In the next chapter we are going to learn how to guard ourselves from smooth prophetic sayings as we discover their potential danger to prophetic operations.

CHAPTER 7

ORDER NOT CONTROL

Our society is filled with those that come into our churches who have formerly opened themselves up to New Age mysticism, witchcraft, the occult, and spiritualism. To protect the flock from false anointings and familiar spirits, there is a proper order in which the Holy Spirit likes to flow.

Where the Spirit of the Lord is there is liberty (2 Corinthians 3:17). However that is not to say that one has the freedom to do just whatever he or she wants to do during a church service. God's word says, "Let all things be done decently and in order (*taxis*)." From the Greek word taxis we get our English word taxi. Taxis means...

a class act through a proper flow.

A PROPER FLOW

Our society is filled with those that come into our churches who have formerly opened themselves up to New Age mysticism, witchcraft, the occult, and spiritualism both knowingly and unknowingly. Because of this, it is very important that these be taught to submit to the order of the house.

> "Wherefore, brethren, covet to prophesy, and forbid not to speak with tongues. {40} Let all things be done decently and in order." (1 Corinthians 14:39-40 KJV)

In order to continue to reverence our God and flow in the liberty of the Holy Spirit, I submit to you that there is a proper order in which the Holy Spirit likes to flow that protects the flock from false anointings and familiar spirits.

With any move, revival, or prophetic voice from the Holy Spirit, it is the responsibility of the local pastors to see to it that the move is received, encouraged, and guided in properly. The house of the Lord must be prepared. (See the pattern Exodus 25:40, 1 Chronicles 28:10-12). With this in mind, any move of or from the Holy Spirit will be to create strong stable Christians, not flaky non-relatable ones. Therefore, spiritual submission to the "order" or "flow" of the house always brings about a spiritual stability that guards the flocks from false anointings.

GUIDELINES
FOR A CLASS FLOW

We are not ignorant of the devil's devices sent to destroy that which God is doing in our midst (2 Corinthians 2:11). Because of the supernatural spiritual nature of Spirit filled church services and because mature spiritual discernment is a must, we offer the following guidelines for worship in our services (Hebrews 5:13-14).

GOD SAID

You have probably heard someone declare that "God said." It is stated so much by some, that we become callous to the saying and don't really pay much attention to it. There are many times when God does prophetically speak to us, yet there are countless times when God really did not say anything at all. Later in this chapter we will give examples of people that have used those words, "God said," inappropriately.

THE PROPHECY OF NATHAN

Remember when Nathan prophesied to King David and said, "Thou art the man?" (2 Samuel 12). Had King David not have personally known the Prophet Nathan he may very well have had him killed for saying those words. But because Nathan was a recognized prophetic voice in David's life, he received Nathan and the prophetic voice.

RECOGNIZED PROPHETIC MINISTRY

Once I attended a special service that a pastor friend had invited me to taking along a person from our ministry. Later that night, we were invited to have dinner in a private setting with some very well known (what I would refer to as veteran) ministry gifts. The person that was with me continued to feel that he had a prophetic word for the pastor and asked me if he could deliver it. My response was emphatically, "No!" Now I know that there are many reading this book that would disagree with me about this. After all, this brother had a "Word." So if he had one, then why couldn't he just go ahead and deliver it? First of all, this brother was submitting his prophecy to his covering (protection), his pastor. Secondly, I did not have a witness to that "Word." Next, the timing was totally inappropriate. Finally, he would not have been received as a prophetic voice since he was totally unknown to those pastors. When it comes to personal prophecy, prophetic ministry gifts are better received when they are recognized as being sent from the Lord.

KNOW THOSE THAT LABOR AMONG YOU

It is important for us to obey the Word. The Bible commands us to "Know those that labor among you." And that would be in a prophetic sense as well.

> "And we beseech you, brethren, to know them which labor among you, and are over you in the Lord, and admonish you"
> (1 Thessalonians 5:12 KJV).

It is important to understand that if a person is truly a ministry gift from God, set into the local church, that ministry gift must be recognized as such by the local pastor or set man. If the local pastor or set man does not recognize that individual as a prophetic gift, then that individual is not sent as a prophetic voice to that particular congregation. I submit this as a proper flow or order.

107

BEWARE OF FALSE PROPHETS

"Beware of false prophets, which come to you in sheep's clothing, but inwardly they are ravening wolves. {16} Ye shall know them by their fruits" (Matthew 7:15-16a KJV).

There are those who come like sheep to our churches and act like prophets who are really ravening wolves. How can we discern them? We can discern them by their fruits. It takes time to know people in such a way as to be able to determine their fruit. The only thing that seems to grow fast in a garden is weeds. We are not judging one's salvation, but we are inspecting their fruit.

Pastors are required to know their flock. This also includes those whom he allows to prophetically labor among it.

"Be thou diligent to know the state of thy flocks, and look well to thy herds." (Proverbs 27:23 KJV)

SENT TO CAUSE DIVISION

"I appeal to you, brethren, to be on your guard concerning those who create dissensions and dif-

ficulties and cause divisions, in
opposition to the doctrine (the
teaching) which you have been
taught. [I warn you to turn aside
from them, to] avoid them. {18}
For such persons do not serve
our Lord Christ but their own
appetites and base desires, and
by ingratiating (good words)
and flattering speech, they be-
guile (deceive) the hearts of the
unsuspecting and simple-
minded [people]." (Romans
16:17-18 AMP)

There is a lot of personal prophecy that
is nothing more than smooth sayings, witchcraft, or those prophesying out of their own
imaginations. When the Holy Spirit speaks
it will be expressly. Whatever God reveals
can be understood by man.

"Now the Spirit *speaketh expressly*, that in the latter times
some shall depart from the faith,
giving heed to seducing spirits,
and doctrines of devils." (1
Timothy 4:1 KJV Italics added)

The manifestation of the Holy Spirit
through prophecy will exalt the Lordship of
Christ and not man. We urge "extreme cau-

tion" in being led by personal prophecies, visions or dreams, and encourage you to submit them to the pastors to draw upon the "safety net" of their experience and spiritual discernment.

Countless times, I have seen good Christian people blow it in prophetic ministry. I have seen both great things and terrible things happen. Every time something terrible happened it was because the hearer refused to allow the prophetic word to be judged.

Many come into our services and pray with us only to tell us that God showed them this or God showed them that. Let's not be afraid to judge every prophetic word.

DARK SAYINGS AND VISIONS

I define dark sayings and visions as those things which are symbolic prophetic pictures. Many times people call me to discuss their visions, dreams or prophecies. I am adamant that our God is perfectly capable of making himself expressly known. God does not give us visions or prophecies of which we cannot know the meaning. Because of the spiritual nature of prophetic words, they need to be interpreted. Knowing how much caution needs to be applied to these words, it only stands to reason that symbolic dreams and visions would require even more caution.

DREAMS

It is difficult to understand why some people have so many dreams that they think are from God. I am not saying that there are not dreams that are from God; there surely are, but every night? Let me try to explain what might be happening to some at night while they sleep.

We willfully choose to serve our God each day. When we sleep at night our will is relaxed and we enter a dream-type state where our body shuts down to sleep. Our spirit (pneuma) is like a filter that picks up on things in the spirit-realm throughout the day or even around us at night. It is these things that we pick up, in our spirits, that we may be seeing in that sleepy realm. But if they are dark sayings that need to be interpreted, they are probably just things that are being filtered out. If you are having symbolic dreams, just wake up and discern them. If you don't "know" what they mean, forget them. Wash everything with the Word of God. The spirit of man "knows" the things of God. The soul man "wonders" about the things of God. Don't call everyone in the church, or look for a "Joseph" to interpret them, and certainly don't share them with everyone you meet. Remember our God is not weird; he is perfectly capable of making himself expressly known.

IMAGINATIONS

I have had people tell me that they have seen visions of everything from spiders to little chicks. They declare, "God showed me this" and "God showed me that." Sadly to say, most of the time they are seeing nothing more than what is coming from their own imaginations.

I don't want to discourage good Christian people who want to grow in the things of the Lord. We want them to blossom in their respective callings and prophetic ministries. However it is important that they are raised up right, being able to know the difference between vain imaginations and true prophetic operations.

Let me attempt to describe what might be happening. If I were to say, "Dog," then you would see a picture of a dog in your mind. You would not see the letters d - o - g. If I were to say, "Tree," then you would see a picture of a tree in your mind. You would not see the letters t - r - e - e. What's the point? People think and see in pictures. That is the way that God created us.

The word says that the manifestation of the Spirit is given to profit withal. To one is given the word of wisdom, to another the word of knowledge, etc. (1 Corinthians 12). It does not say, to one is given the manifestation of a "picture" of knowledge, or a "picture" of wisdom.

GOD USES PROPHETS
TO UNLOCK TIMES AND SEASONS

Therefore what is happening to many well intentioned, loving Christians is that they are seeing pictures, conceived in their own imagination, that are nothing more than how God designed them to see while hearing what is said.

The danger is when they tell others that God showed them this, or God showed them that. It may be nothing more than pictures seen inside one's own imagination, functioning the very way that God made it to function. This should stress again the importance of having the unction (permission to speak) of the Holy Spirit before saying, "God said or God showed me."

SEVEN EXAMPLES
OF IMAGINATIONS

Now let me give you some examples of people who have had a word picture in their imaginations and told others that it was God.

1. A CHANGE OF MIND

One person told me that God sent them to the grocery store to purchase a certain product. Upon arrival they found that the store was out of stock on that product. They told me that God then spoke again saying, "Now go over to the other store, and they will have it." Was God really not aware of where that product was? Did God just simply change his mind or did this person never hear from God to start with? I hope you chose the latter.

2. THUS SAITH THE LORD

A pastor friend in Amsterdam Holland told the story of a person who stood up in his church declaring, "Thus saith the Lord. Just as Noah led the children out of Egypt ..... silence ..... Thus saith the Lord, I made a mistake ...... Just as Moses ...."

3. GOD TOLD ME TO TELL YOU TO READ THIS

One time I was standing on the platform during a service with my eyes closed during worship. A lady left her seat and headed toward me. Upon reaching me she plunged her Bible into my stomach, startling me, and said, "Here, God told me to tell you to read this Psalm right now!" I responded by saying, "Not now, go and sit back down." She was highly offended and left the church in a huff, never to be seen again. Did God really speak to her?

4. YOU'RE GOING TO DIE

A certain man was not acknowledged as a prophetic ministry gift at our church, Spirit of Life Ministries in Hallandale Beach Florida. He then said to me, "Thus saith the Lord, because you have not acknowledged me as your personal prophet you will die in thirty days." This was a sad day for me. I was forced to deal very sternly with this man.

5. YOU DON'T HAVE TO WORK

Another person said that "God told him" that he did not have to work because he was to live a total life of faith. We found that he was some fifty years old, living off of his mother's social security and that he had put

115

his foreign wife out to work on his behalf. This man was using "God said" as an excuse for laziness.

6. THROWN OUT

Another person wanted to give a prophecy that was not in the right flow of the church service. When told that he was not allowed to deliver it right then, he stood and began to publicly and loudly cast the devil out of the pastor. He was thrown out of the church by the ushers.

7. REBUKE YOUR PASTOR

A man showed me a video where a "Prophet," through prophesy, told him to go and rebuke his pastor and set him in order. He asked me to judge this prophesy, and, of course, I told him that he did not have any authority to rebuke his pastor and that the prophesy was not from God. The man then got very angry with me and told me that I needed deliverance. Funny though, if I would have agreed with the prophecy then I would not have needed deliverance.

All of these are real life examples of Christians who have violated their Christian witness. We love them, yet we must maintain an atmosphere of order and proper taxis in our churches. Our God is not a flake. By maintaining the proper flow and order in the house of God we collectively raise up prophetic ministry to be more accurate.

"God showed me this, God said that, I saw this, I dreamed that," etc. Please wait until you are recognized by the leadership of your local church before publicly declaring your spiritual experiences. Most pastors want you to blossom in ministry, but they want to raise you up right. If you have a "prophetic word," first get permission from the pastor to share it until such a time as your ministry is recognized within that local church.

At Spirit of Life Ministries we encourage the activation of prophetic ministry but we also judge all prophecy, dreams, and visions without being offended.

NO PRIVATE MINISTRY PLEASE

Some groups are notorious for having their "own thing" going own during a church service. It's as if God is dividing his focus. During services it is important to get into agreement with your pastor. Don't lay hands and pray or prophesy for someone while the service is in progress. No private ministry please. Maintain an atmosphere of faith, reverence, worship, agreement, and expectation.

117

DEMONS & DELIVERANCE

During times of deliverance, stay in your seat and don't touch people who are being prayed for. We had a lady in our church who was slain in the Spirit and laying on the floor. Her friend that brought her to church started to go and pick her up off the floor and help her back to her seat. The ushers saw her and stopped her because they knew that God was not finished with her. A few moments later this lady was delivered from the hold of an evil spirit. Had her friend succeeded in taking her back to her seat too soon, it's likely that she would have robbed her of her deliverance.

SUMMARY

❏The Greek word taxis (order) means a class act through a proper flow (2 Corinthians 3:17).

❏Prophetic ministry gifts are better received when they are recognized as being sent from the Lord. If a person is truly a ministry gift from God, set into a local church, that ministry gift must be recognized as such by the local pastor or set man.

□If the local pastor or set man does not recognize that individual as a prophetic gift, then that individual is not sent as a prophetic voice to that particular congregation.

□The Holy Spirit speaks expressly (1 Timothy 4:1). To speak expressly means in a plain and definite way.

In the next chapter we will look at the difference between spiritualism and the Holy Spirit as we review the earmarks of a spiritist.

CHAPTER 8

EARMARKS OF A SPIRITIST

Spiritualism is the counterfeit of the Holy Spirit. A spiritist is one who operates inside the spirit realm without the Holy Spirit. How do we tell the difference between spiritualism and the Holy Spirit?

O ver the last few years I have noticed an increase in spiritualism trying to operate in churches. Just because something sounds spiritual doesn't necessarily mean that it is of God. Just because someone says, "Thus saith the Lord, or I saw this, or I heard that," doesn't mean that it is the Spirit of God. It could simply be his or her own imagination at work.

It is important for the prophetic church to be able to understand the difference between spiritualism and the Holy Spirit. In this chapter we will look at the characteristics of spiritualism. Just because someone has a prophetic label doesn't mean that they have the accurate goods.

Spiritualism is the counterfeit of the Holy Spirit. For example fortune telling is the counterfeit of the foretelling of prophetic operations. Physic healing is the counterfeit of God's healing power. For almost every true gift and flow of God, there is a demonic counterfeit.

A spiritist is one who operates inside the spirit realm without the Holy Spirit. By their wills and help from familiar spirits, they choose to go into the spirit realm without God.

The closer we get to the end of the age the more we will see an increase in the operation of spiritualism, even operating inside of our churches. This devil of spiritualism likes to hang out in church because that is an area where it can express itself.

Those that have the most difficulty with spiritualism are those who operate in the prophetic. There are those who want to flow prophetically in what I call deep dark sayings. They are not called but they chase spiritual experiences fueled by their own personal spiritual pride, desiring to operate in prophetic utterances so as to be seen of men.

> "But there were false prophets also among the people, even as there shall be false teachers among you, who privily shall bring in damnable heresies,

even denying the Lord that bought them, and bring upon themselves swift destruction." (2 Peter 2:1 KJV)

Peter is not speaking of those outside the church in this scripture. Peter is saying that there was, and will continue to be a false prophetic voice among the people. Notice the word prophet. He was referring to a false prophetic operation in their midst. Those operating in spiritualism will always seek to enter prophetic ministry whether in the delivery, carrying, or the receiving end. Now I believe strongly in the true prophetic operations of the Spirit of God, but we must address the false too just as Peter did.

"Follow after charity, and desire spiritual gifts, but rather that ye may prophesy. {2} For he that speaketh in an unknown tongue speaketh not unto men, but unto God: for no man understandeth him; howbeit in the spirit he speaketh mysteries. {3} But he that prophesieth speaketh unto men to edification, and exhortation, and comfort." (1 Corinthians 14:1-3 KJV)

123

This verse is a great key to understanding prophetic utterances. Prophecy should edify and build up its hearers. It should not be a prophecy that releases instability or confusion. Whatever God reveals, one should be able to understand. Prophecy should build you up and strengthen you to fight the good fight of faith. It should be fuel to strengthen you and encourage you to keep on going.

Prophecy should give you a knowing in your heart and not a wondering in your head. We have heard some ask, "I wonder what that prophetic word meant?" Some prophecies are so unclear that many ask everyone in the church for an interpretation. Our God is not a flake; he is perfectly capable of making himself very clear. Prophecy should encourage the hearer with a divine exhortation that comforts them.

I have heard people say that they saw big spiders around someone. Or that they saw black rivers and things of that sort. That is not comforting. True prophecy always builds up the church and never feeds the spiritual pride of others.

14 EARMARKS
OF A SPIRITIST

Spiritualism is the counterfeit of the Holy Spirit. Let's look at fourteen earmarks of a spiritist through the teaching of the Apostle Peter's letter to the church.

1. Private Ministry

> "But there were false prophets also among the people, even as there shall be false teachers among you, who privily shall bring in damnable heresies, even denying the Lord that bought them, and bring upon themselves swift destruction." (2 Peter 2:1 KJV Italics added)

The first earmark of a spiritist is private ministry. They will try to isolate you from others. There prophetic operations are 'too deep' for everyone in the church except their victims. They look for those that they can prophesy to privately. At some point, these operators of spiritualism will work their way into false doctrine through so called pro-phetic operations.

2. Pernicious

> "And many shall follow their pernicious ways; by reason of whom the way of truth shall be evil spoken of." (2 Peter 2:2 KJV Italics added)

Pernicious ways lead to spiritual destruction. Perniciousness will cause...

injury

destruction

ruin

fatalities.

Those that fall prey to spiritualism learn to follow the ways of the spiritist (the false prophet). They even go so far as to dress alike, wear their hair the same way, and all their mannerisms look the same. Even their accents sound the same. False prophets make cookie-cutters of themselves. When you look closely at their lives you will find a trail of damaged relationships and people they have hurt severally.

3. Merchandisers

> "And through covetousness
> shall they with feigned (fabri-
> cated) words make merchandise
> of you: whose judgment now of
> a long time lingereth not, and
> their damnation slumbereth
> not." (2 Peter 2:3 KJV)

Those operating in spiritualism use manipulation and control through false prophecy to merchandise people. They will use
smooth prophetic utterances to get you to
do their will. There are those who will say
that they saw or heard something from God
and prophesy with underlying motives to
control you. Prophetic control is the worst
of evils.

4. Unclean

> "But chiefly them that walk af-
> ter the flesh in the lust of un-
> cleanness" (2 Peter 2:10 KJV).

Spiritist are unclean. The Greek word for
unclean is *miasmes* meaning the act of defiling or polluting. Not only are they themselves defiled but they choose to pollute you
as well.

5. Despise Governments

"...despise government" (2 Peter
2:10 KJV).

Those who walk in spiritualism despise
governments. To despise means to think
little or nothing of. They say things like, "I
am submitted to the Holy Spirit only and I
will only do what he says." Their rebellion
drives them to attack all in authority. The
Holy Spirit seems to take them all over town
and they never plug into any local church
ministry. They are accountable to no one.

Spiritist despise God's five-fold government. They say things like, "Don't you dare
tell me what to do! I can worship God my
own way. I have a 'home' church. I had someone from India lay hands on me and confirm me the pastor. Who does that pastor
think he is! I'm going to run to this conference and that meeting and I am going to get
sister so-and-so to lay hands on me and
prophesy smooth sayings over me and tell
me how wonderful I am. I will never allow
that pastor to bring correction in my life."

6. Presumptuous And Self-willed

"Presumptuous are they, self-
willed" (2 Peter 2:10 KJV).

A presumptuous person is too bold or forward. They take too much for granted and have an overconfident and arrogant air about them. They are full of self-will and say to themselves, "I'm not going to crucify my flesh because I am my own god." One controlled by self-will is his own god. It means that he can do anything he wants to, at anytime he wants to.

Spiritualist are very self-centered and answerable to no one. Those who operate out of spiritualism will not be submissive unless it's beneficial to them. A presumptuous prophet is one that thinks he should prophesy just because he can by his own will. Those who are into spiritualism do things at their own will, without the unction (permission) of the Holy Spirit. If you don't have the unction, keep your mouth shut.

7. Speak Evil Of Authority

> "speak evil of dignities (authority)" (2 Peter 2:10 KJV).

The five-fold ministry gifts have been given spiritual and natural authority. Those that flow in spiritualism are not afraid to sit around the coffee table and talk evil of their ministers. "I just didn't get a witness about that minister. He's into hyper-faith and spiritual warfare. Who does he think he is?"

129

Spiritualism likes to take the devil's lies and just pass them out to everyone. Those involved in spiritualism build their own disciples outside the local church.

8. Speak Of Things They Know Nothing About

> "But these, as natural brute beasts, made to be taken and destroyed, speak evil of the things that they understand not; and shall utterly perish in their own corruption." (2 Peter 2:12 KJV)

Those that are spiritist try to make others think that they are real deep, spiritually. I heard a lady say one time to another, "You are so deep in the spirit. I just don't know how you get back when you get out there so far."

9. Sporting Themselves

> "And shall receive the reward of unrighteousness, as they that count it pleasure to riot in the day time. Spots they are and blemishes, sporting themselves

with their own deceivings while
they feast with you." (2 Peter
2:13 KJV Italics added)

The spiritist plays a game of deceit and
cannot even be honest with himself. He
sports about bragging on how much he is
involved in and how wonderful he is. This
reminds me of a peacock that would visit
my back yard from time to time. He would
spread his tail feathers and sport himself
around the yard. As he fanned his feathers
he would sport himself about, acting like
the yard was his.

10. Sexual Sins

"Having eyes full of adultery,
and that cannot cease from sin"
(2 Peter 2:14 KJV).

Everyone that I ever met who operated in
spiritualism had some sort of problem with
sexual sin. I guarantee you that they cannot cease from sin because their hearts are
full of lust.

11. Deceiving The Unstable

"beguiling unstable souls" (2
Peter 2:14 KJV).

Those who are into false operations look for unstable souls. People that aren't stable are those who are not submissive or plugged in. They are those who have trouble remaining stable. They might be real melancholy in their character or real "woe is me," even somewhat schizophrenic. But they are definitely those who struggle in the soulish realm. Your soul is your will, mind, emotions, intellect, reasoning, and imagination.

Spiritism looks to create soul ties. They will play on what's hurting you and bothering you. Just remember you can't flatter a stable person. The compliment we want is when Jesus says, "Well done thou good and faithful servant" (Matthew 25:21).

12. Covetous Practices

> "an heart they have exercised with covetous practices; cursed children." (2 Peter 2:14 KJV)

This spirit is after your possessions, "If I could just have your money, your husband, your ministry, your etc." A pastor told me that he overheard someone saying, "it would be nice to be a pastor's wife." The problem was that this woman was already married. Her statement was made out of the wrong spirit.

13. Forsaken The Right Way

"Which have forsaken the right way, and are gone astray, following the way of Balaam the son of Bosor, who loved the wages of unrighteousness; {16} But was rebuked for his iniquity: the dumb ass speaking with man's voice forbad the madness of the prophet. {17} These are wells without water, clouds that are carried with a tempest; to whom the mist of darkness is reserved for ever."
(2 Peter 2:15-17 KJV)

Spiritist try to make it happen or work things up. You don't have to help God. The Holy Spirit knows what He's doing. Balaam was taken captive by the idolatry in his heart and became a merchandiser of the anointing.

14. Great Swelling Smooth Words

"For when they speak great swelling words of vanity, they allure through the lusts of the flesh, through much wantonness, those that were clean escaped from them who live in error." (2 Peter 2:18 KJV)

133

Spiritist lure others through the lust of the flesh saying things like, "God wants to make you a big man." They know how to feed your spiritual pride and pull on any common ground that you might have through the lust for things.

> "While they promise them liberty, they themselves are the servants of corruption: for of whom a man is overcome, of the same is he brought in bondage." (2 Peter 2:19 KJV)

I hope that you have come to the conclusion that it is possible for a true prophetic gifting to tap into a false prophetic operation.

Prophetic Operations was written to discuss the vulnerability of the prophet only in an attempt to hold the prophetic gift and the "Word of the Lord" in high esteem. It is up to the prophetic leadership to examine itself in the possibility of being defiled by false prophetic operations, as well as the possibility of defiling others.

With every great move of the Spirit, there is a time of preparation and understanding of how to relate, flow, and function in that gifting. We should come to the conclusion that even though we have the ability to prophesy by faith, we need to understand that it is extremely important to...

> examine our motives before the Lord

> wait for the safety of an unction or the prompting of the Holy Spirit.

One final thought. If the people of God do not respond properly to God's prophetic flow and they attempt to use prophetic gifting for self-advancement, manipulation, merchandising and control, or if the prophet's office is coveted only for personal prophecy rather than, "What saith the Spirit of the Lord to the church," then I believe the prophetic ministry will be impeded severely and many will become discouraged and some even lost. But if the church will allow the prophetic gifting to function the way God designed it, then the church will prosper and continue to grow in that which only the prophetic anointing provides.

SUMMARY

☐Spiritualism is the counter-feit of the Holy Spirit.

☐A spiritist is one who operates inside the spirit realm without the Holy Spirit.

☐Whatever God reveals, one should be able to understand.

☐The first earmark of a spirit-ist is private ministry.

☐Prophetic control is the worst of evils.

☐Balaam was taken captive by the idolatry in his heart and became a merchandiser of the anointing.

☐Spiritist despise authority and refuse to submit.

THE PATTERN OF THE SPIRITIST

☐Despise government.

☐Presumptuous.

☐Self-willed.

☐Speak evil of authority.

☐Speak of that they don't understand.

☐Play games with themselves.

☐ Full of adultery (hidden sexual sins).

☐Prostitute themselves with false motives.

☐Spiritual pride.

☐Charming, flattering smooth sayings.

☐Looking for unstable souls.

☐Full of covetousness.

☐Following after Balaam (unrighteous riches).

137

☐ Speak great swelling words of vanity.

☐ Allure through the lust of the flesh, pride and riches.

☐ Promise liberty with their teachings, but they only bind you up with control.

☐ Seldom address sin.

☐ Full of manipulation and control.

☐ Buck, fight and attack spiritual authority.

☐ Draw people to themselves (will not build the local church).

☐ Will prophesy without the unction (permission) of the Spirit, according to their own will.

☐ They go out into the spirit realm without God.

☐ Have an air of superiority about them.

☐Full of pride, not humility and meekness.

☐Work on your emotions, looking for soulish areas to create soul ties.

☐Push open doors that they have no business pushing open.

☐Full of false motives.

☐Feed spiritual pride, and pull on the common ground of lust.

☐Feed idolatry.

Woman on the Beast

"And there came one of the seven angels which had the seven vials, and talked with me, saying unto me, Come hither; I will show unto thee the judgment of the great whore that sitteth upon many waters: {2} With whom the kings of the earth have committed fornication, and the inhabitants of the earth have been made drunk with the wine of her fornication. {3} So he carried me away in the spirit into the wilderness: and I saw a woman sit upon a scarlet-colored beast, full of names of blasphemy, having seven heads and ten horns. {4} And the woman was arrayed in purple and scarlet color, and decked with gold and precious stones and pearls, having a golden cup in her hand full of abominations and filthiness of her fornication: {5} And upon her forehead was a name written, MYSTERY, BABYLON THE GREAT, THE MOTHER OF HARLOTS AND ABOMINATIONS OF THE EARTH. {6} And I saw the woman drunken with the blood of the saints, and with the blood of the martyrs of Jesus: and when I saw her, I wondered with great admiration." (Revelation 17:1-6 KJV

INDEX

142

Witchcraft. 65
Woe 13
Wolves 108
Wonders 111
Wooden idols 58, 74
Word of the Lord 6
Word to the church 9
Worldliness 23

Y

Yoking with idols 24
Young prophets 6

Z

Zedekiah 82, 88
Zippor 54

INVITATION

Hello friends and partners!

In addition to preaching the gospel around the world, we also have a powerful church in South Florida and would love to have you visit with us. The Spirit of God told us to start a church and raise up people in strength and power who would reach their city and impact the nations. SOLM has an international apostolic and prophetic call, as well as a mandate to raise up a strong local church by ministering to the whole family. SOLM has the reputation of being a place where you can receive what you need from the Lord; whether it be healing, miracles, deliverance, restoration, victory, or success. Why? Because with God all things are possible. SOLM' uniqueness is being recognized and sought after as we continue growing in spiritual liberty, influence, strength and power. We invite you to come and receive confirmation, impartation, and activation.

In the Master's service,
Jonas and Rhonda Clark

EXPOSING SPIRITUAL WITCHCRAFT

Spiritual witch-craft is the power of Satan. Its purpose is to control and ma-nipulate you.

The weapons of witchcraft are emo-tional manipulation, spiritual and reli-gious control, isolation, soul ties, fear, con-fusion, loss of personal identity, sickness, depression and prophetic divination.

Those caught in the snare of this spirit struggle all their Christian life to remain stable in their walk with Christ.

Topics include: the character of spiritual witchcraft, the weapons of witchcraft, the road to deception and lastly — breaking free!

"I fought this spirit from April to November and won. So can you!"

ISBN 1-886885-00-1

JEZEBEL SEDUCING GODDESS OF WAR

Jezebel is the warrior goddess who has gone unchallenged in our generation. Dr. Lester Sumrall said that she would be the greatest opposer of the apostolic church before the coming of the Lord. In 1933 Voice of Healing Prophet William Branham had a vision of her rising to take control.

"Some people write about things that they know nothing about. Not this time! It is time to barbecue this spirit."

ISBN 1-886885-04-4

50 EARMARKS OF AN APOSTOLIC CHURCH

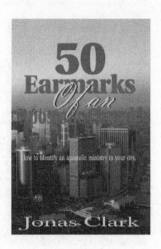

Jesus said, "I will build my church and the gates of hell shall not prevail." So what kind of church is it that Jesus is building? Is it a religious church? A traditional church? A defeated church? Or is it a glorious church without spot or wrinkle?

Right now we are experiencing an awesome paradigm shift in ministry. The Holy Spirit is moving us into a time of the restoration of the apostolic ministry. All over the world God is birthing apostolic churches. But what do they look like? What makes them so different? Is there one in your city? In this thought-provoking book Jonas teaches you 50 earmarks of an apostolic church in your city. It's time to cross the bridge into the apostolic. Are you ready to be a part of an exciting glorious church?

ISBN 1-886885-06-0

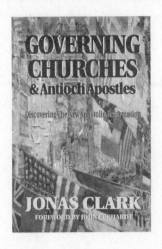

GOVERNING CHURCHES & ANTIOCH APOSTLES

Apostolic churches build, guide, govern, blast, establish, carry liberty, impart blessing, set, father, mature, set the pace, influence, train, send, launch, hear, say and do.

A new move of the Holy Spirit has begun! It is the call for a new apostolic reformation. This reformation is challenging old religious structures and systems. It is restoring the understanding of an apostolic church that will enable us to fulfill the great commission. It's time to discover your role in the new apostolic reformation.

ISBN 1-886885-07-9

IMAGINATIONS DON'T LIVE THERE!

Have you floated out into an imagination today? The Word of God teaches us to be led by the Spirit of God. However, we must first learn how to conquer the weird world of soulish imaginations. An imagination is a picture conceived in the spirit of one's mind that forms a mental picture of what is not. Imaginations speak of things that haven't happened and are not real. Once spoken they come alive. When acted on they lead to fear, instability, and feelings of insecurity. The freedom to imagine must first be fortified with truth. This book will help you take control of your mind and free you to be led by the Spirit of God.

ISBN 1-886885-03-6

COME OUT!

It is time for the church to exercise her authority against Satan who has been allowed to maintain his oppression without a challenge. In this handbook for the serious deliverance minister we will study...

the scriptural foundations for deliverance

how to continue the deliverance ministry of Jesus

the different types of spirits mentioned in the Bible

how to cast out devils

six things evil spirits attach themselves to

how to keep our deliverance

and much more.

ISBN 1-886885-10-0

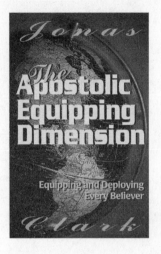

APOSTOLIC EQUIPPING DIMENSION

The Lord Jesus is our pattern for the greatest of all apostolic leaders. He took twelve ordinary men with various personalities, weaknesses, flaws and strengths and transformed them into a dynamic, world-changing revolutionary team.

This book is about entering the fascinating realm of the apostolic dimension. In this realm the Holy Spirit will set, refresh, equip and deploy you into the exciting world of ministry. The ministry belongs to you. Are you ready to find your purpose and enter your destiny?

ISBN 1-886885-08-7

RELIGIOUS SPIRITS

One of the most deadly influences in the body of Christ today is the religious spirit.

Religious people themselves have been used as the devil's assassins, targeting the spiritually young, the zealous, the hungry and the leadership.

This book will speak into the lives of those who are being spiritually abused by religious spirits who steal the spiritual zeal from God-called, anointed, and appointed children of God.

All of us have experienced the onslaught of the religious spirit in our lives. This book will open the eyes of those who themselves have been seduced into religious forms and traditions of men, and offer them a way out of carnal religious activity.

ISBN 1-886885-12-5

Global Cause Network

THE GLOBAL CAUSE NETWORK is a network of churches and ministries that have united together to build a platform for an apostolic voice. The *GCN* is built on relationships rather than denominational politics. It consists of those who recognize the importance of apostolic gifts working together with all five ascension gifts to equip believers for the work of ministry. By uniting we have forged an alliance across the globe that is building a 'great net for a great catch.' The foundational vision of the *GCN* is covenant relationships between its membership for the advancement of the gospel of Jesus Christ throughout the world.

MISSION STATEMENT

• To reach the world with the gospel of Jesus Christ.

• To build and strengthen the local church.

THE GLOBAL CAUSE NETWORK PROVIDES...

• apostolic and prophetic identity with a strong sense of community

• a platform to coordinate, enhance and release God's apostolic and prophetic voice

• a focus to impact our cities and the nations with the gospel

• apostolic covering, confirmation, impartation, activation, team ministry, sending, church planting and release of ministry gifts

• critical learning resources, educational and informational materials vital to the advancement of the network

• apostolic fathering, focus and direction

• facilitation of relationship by connecting those of like precious faith together

For more information contact the GCN ministry office.

The Global Cause Network
Apostle Jonas Clark
27 West Hallandale Beach Blvd
Hallandale, Florida
33009
(954) 456-4420

email: life@catchlife.org
Web site www.catchlife.org

MINISTRY INFORMATION

For a complete ministry catalog of tapes, books and videos, or to invite Jonas to speak at your next conference, please contact

Spirit of Life Ministries
27 West Hallandale Beach Blvd.
Hallandale, Florida 33009
(954) 456-4420

email: life@catchlife.org

BOOKS
BY JONAS CLARK

Jezebel, Seducing Goddess of War

Exposing Spiritual Witchcraft

Apostolic Equipping Dimension

Come Out!

Governing Churches & Antioch Apostles

50 Earmarks of an Apostolic Church

Imaginations, Don't Live There!

Prophetic Operations

Religious Spirits

Available in
quality Christian bookstores or
easy on-line internet ordering
http://catchlife.org or call toll free
(800) 943-6490

Spirit of Life Ministries
27 West Hallandale Beach Blvd.
Hallandale, Florida 33009
(954) 456-4420

email: life@catchlife.org